This Book Is Dedicated to the Memory of My Parents,

Charles and Helen Frankel

Praise for Out of the Labyrinth

"*Out of the Labyrinth* is one of those breakthrough books that puts things into perspective. Carl Frankel has given me the vocabulary and concepts to see what's going on." -Stuart Auchincloss, board member, CERES

"This is the work of a first-class, learned mind and a sensitive spirit. These qualities combine to draw me into Frankel's thought and take me to a place of vision, clarity and, yes, wisdom far beyond my own. This is a magnificent book and extremely important reading for anyone who yearns for a better world." -Ray Anderson, chairman, Interface Flooring Company

"*Out of the Labyrinth* reflects a journey that is both personal and global toward the path of sustainability. It is a story of the search for an integral vision that is moving in its authenticity and compelling in its call for honoring the depth dimensions of ourselves. It is a book to be read with profit by all who are seeking a sustainable future for people and the planet."
-Mary Evelyn Tucker, co-director, Forum on Religion and Ecology

"Written from a deeply philosophical stance, the book is at the same time accessible and practical. Frankel shows us the potential power of post-modern thinking without falling into the negative and nihilistic stance adopted by so many critics of the current state of the world. For anyone committed to positive change in the world, *Out of the Labyrinth* should find a spot in their library." -John R. Ehrenfeld, Director Emeritus, MIT Technology, Business and Environment Program

To John —
With warm
regards and best wishes
for a happy and integral
future

Rochester NY
November 2005

Carl

OUT OF THE LABYRINTH

Out of the Labyrinth

*Who We Are, How We Go Wrong
And
What We Can Do About It*

Carl Frankel

Monkfish Book Publishing Company
Rhinebeck, New York

Library of Congress Cataloging-in-Publication Data

Frankel, Carl.
  Out of the labyrinth : who we are, how we go wrong, and what we can do about it / by Carl Frankel.
      p. cm.
  Includes bibliographical references.
  ISBN 0-9726357-6-9
  1. Culture. 2. Social history--20th century. I. Title.
  HM621.F73 2004
  306--dc22

                              2004000671

Book and cover design by Georgia Dent
Cover art: Getty Images

Bulk purchase discounts, for educational or promotional purposes are available. Contact the publisher for more information.

First edition

First impression

10 9 8 7 6 5 4 3 2 1

Monkfish Book Publishing Company
27 Lamoree Road
Rhinebeck, NY 12572
monkfishpublishing.com

Acknowledgments

Late one evening in March 1999, I had a passing thought about the categories of activity that occupy our lives. It didn't feel especially unusual, except for one thing: the thought stayed with me. Over the weeks that followed, it evolved into something of an *idée fixe*. By June, I was so consumed by the material churning around in my head that I decided it had to become a book. I told my wife it was all quite clear and straightforward and that I could easily hammer it out in three months, four at most. Five years, four name changes, and eight drafts later, I finally had a work that felt ready for publication. Some books, I'm told, pop out easily. This one didn't.

It was a long and bumpy road I traveled, and I only reached the end of it with the support and guidance of a great many friends and colleagues along the way. Pat Anderson, Stuart Auchincloss, Barbara Bash, Scot Case, Mitchell Ditkoff, Charlie Dorris, John Elkington, Joe Firmage, Aaron Frankel, Ann Graham, Doug Grunther, Paul Hawken, Susan Hunter, Rick Ingrasci, Wendy Klein, Joe Laur, Lysa Leyland, Bob Massie, David McCarthy, Will Nixon, Steve Piersanti, Susan Quasha, Phil Randell, Susan Ray, Ray Rizzo, Brent Robison, Sim Van Der Ryn, Sarah Schley, Chuck Stein, Hudson Talbott, and Martin Wright are among the readers to whom I owe an enormous debt of gratitude. There are times when tough love is the best sort of love, and I got some pretty heavy doses of it along the way.

If I have failed to mention other readers, it is due to a failure of memory, not a lack of gratitude.

I cannot praise highly enough the publishing and editing team that came together toward the end of this journey. Publisher Paul Cohen has proven to be a critical but kind, grounded but supportive, and steadfastly congenial collaborator. Susan Bridle brought superb listening skills, a pitch-perfect editorial eye, and a deep knowledge of integral philosophy to the task of taking the manuscript to the next level. Georgia Dent contributed creativity and commitment to the book's layout and design.

A separate paragraph, maybe an entire ode, is due my wife, Deborah Bansemer, who provided gentle and wise counsel every step of the way. She boosted my spirits when they were down and was forbearing when they were inflated. I cannot imagine having a kinder, more considerate (or fun!) life-companion.

Finally, I would like to thank my mother, Helen Frankel, and my father, Charles Frankel, for having brought me into this world, and for having been the people they were. Where would I be without them? And where would this book be? Over twenty years ago, tragedy cost them their lives. This book is my way of reaching out to them.

"*The problems of our time are ultimately the problems of our own deepest nature.*"

—J. C. Hall

TABLE OF CONTENTS

PROLOGUE:
IN THE LABYRINTH

As a symbol of the human condition, the labyrinth dates back thousands of years. In the Greek myth, Minos, the king of Crete, kept as a pet the Minotaur, a fearsome half man, half bull that he housed in the center of a vast labyrinth built by the legendary architect Daedalus. Minos had a longstanding feud with Athens and required its king, Aigeus, to pay a terrible price to maintain the peace. Every year he was required to send seven boys and seven girls to Crete, where they were sacrificed to the Minotaur. Not a nice fellow, that Minos.

Theseus, the son of King Aigeus, resolved to end this sorry state of affairs by traveling to Crete and slaying the beast. His decision was met with much dismay by the adoring citizens of Athens, but the young prince insisted and set out with the other victims for Minos's kingdom. Upon their arrival, they were paraded through the capital city. It was then that Ariadne, the daughter of King Minos, first laid eyes on Theseus and immediately fell in love. She went to the architect Daedalus and sought guidance on how to save the prince. An Athenian by birth, Daedalus wished Theseus well and came up with an ingenious idea. If the prince fastened a thread to the doorpost at the entrance of the labyrinth and trailed it after him as he made his way into its heart, then he would be able to return again—assuming, of course, that he somehow managed to slay the Minotaur.

Theseus did as he was advised, prevailed in his encounter with the beast, and followed the thread out of the labyrinth to safety. Soon after, he departed Crete, accompanied by the Athenian men and maidens—and by Ariadne.

It is noteworthy that Theseus enters and departs the labyrinth by the same door. So it is for all of us: we enter the labyrinth of life through the door of birth and depart it through the door of death, and although one comes at the beginning and the other at the end of our lives, they are really the same door. Both perform the same function: they separate the known world of our embodied lives from the unknowable world of the beyond.

In addition to being a metaphor for our mortal condition, the labyrinth also symbolizes the search for self—a quest we humans have been on since long before the ancient Greeks. By their nature, myths lend themselves to multiple interpretations, and in the case of the labyrinth, one of them is this: we can only discover our true nature by turning inward. We must explore the depth of our inner experience and intuitions with no one to guide us but ourselves, and this feels like being in a labyrinth. We make wrong turns; we double back on ourselves; we chase chimera and find ourselves unable to find our way to freedom and the light of day. And at the center of the labyrinth there awaits the Minotaur, the one great fear that more than anything blocks our way.

Theseus was a hero because he prevailed in the search for self. He ventured into the depth of his own inner experience, confronted and overcame the Minotaur, his deepest and most paralyzing fear, and then emerged safely into the known world again. He made his way *out* by making his way *back*: he discovered his own true self by returning to his point of origin, to the place he started from. And so the myth of the labyrinth teaches, among other things, that we find out who we really are by setting out on a journey that feels like forward movement but ultimately returns us, if we are successful, to what the poet Edwin Muir, drawing from the Zen tradition, has called our "original face":

> For then we played for victory
> And not to make each other glad.
> A darkness covered every head,
> Frowns twisted the original face,
> And through the mask we could not see,
> The beauty and the buried grace.[1]

Our true and "original" face awaits us. But it takes a journey into the labyrinth, and through our own fear, to find it. We go into the dizzying darkness and make our way back into the light again, which now shines more brightly than it has ever shone before.

In addition to this outcome, which is the hero's absolute victory, there is another, more modest type of victory. It comes when we muster up the courage to confront our deepest fears yet can't quite defeat them. Although this in one sense is a loss, we also win because we have been courageous.

We only know complete defeat when we remain on the sidelines, prisoner to our fears. This is when we know shame. This is when the Minotaur devours us.

ぞぞぞぞぞ

The myth of the labyrinth is more relevant than ever today. In important ways, the labyrinth itself has changed, though. Our latter-day labyrinth is not strictly personal or even local. Our culture is global; our labyrinth now encompasses the entire world. And an especially daunting maze it is, because our world is so much more complex and confusing than the smaller, much more straightforward world of yore. In today's labyrinth, which is so much vaster than the one from olden times, our footsteps echo much more loudly than before.

It is also the case that the Minotaur is especially imposing now. Our instruments of fear and death are so much more powerful than they used to be. Today's Minotaur has nuclear, chemical, and biological weapons at his disposal. And in his eyes, if we look closely enough, we can also see the specter of an ecologically devastated planet, which is what awaits us if we continue on our current trajectory. These are fearsome powers indeed.

This is not to suggest that things are hopeless. Today, as ever, we can prevail against fear and the challenges that confront us. What the mythologist Joseph Campbell called the "hero's journey" remains a viable option. But the obstacles are especially daunting.

As we embark on our journey through this book, it may be

useful to spend a few moments examining what makes our contemporary cultural labyrinth such an especially dizzying place. For starters, there are the ubiquitous forces of *distraction* and *denial*. Our entertainment culture presents us with a dumbed-down version of ourselves; our media culture sells to fear ("If it bleeds it leads" is the motto of broadcast news media); our consumer culture peddles endless trivialities. Each of these forces is potent in its own right and more so in combination. Collectively they create a black-magic spell that is like an occupying army of the spirit. Under the thrall of this "dark enchantment," we lose sight of our highest potential, hunker down inside our anxiety, and try to buy our way to happiness—all false turns in the labyrinth.

A second factor that makes modern society such a terrifying labyrinth is the *rate of change*. We humans are animals, and as animals we evolve at a quite leisurely pace. Darwinian time is slow time: fundamental changes occur over millions of years. But technical knowledge evolves much faster. In the past decade alone, scientific knowledge advanced more than it did during the entire previous history of humanity. And that was just the warm-up act: the years ahead will bring exponentially faster change.

It is difficult, if not impossible, for our animal natures to adapt to this rate of change. With the future constantly pulling the rug of the present out from under our feet, we cannot easily keep our balance—or a level head. The rate of change has us constantly battling, often below conscious awareness, to maintain our equilibrium. And this makes the modern labyrinth an especially dizzying place.

A third consideration is our *globalized postmodern culture*. Life in the "good old days" wasn't necessarily all that good but it was certainly less complicated than the world we know today. Most people never traveled more than a few days' ride from their birthplace during the entire course of their lives. The result was a sharply circumscribed set of options regarding values and identity. People simply put on the clothes they were handed. If you were from Provence, you thought and acted like a Provençal. If you were from Massachusetts, you thought and acted like a Yankee.

Today we can fly to the farthest point on the globe in hours, and we can communicate with anyone, anywhere, instantaneously. As time has accelerated, space has contracted, and this has vastly increased our options regarding what to believe and who to be. If we go into a music store today, we can find reggae music, klezmer music, celtic music, hip-hop music, and innumerable other styles as well. It is similar for our values and self-sense: we can try on what we like and mix and match to our heart's content. If the rate of change is dizzying, our range of choices is, too.

All these factors—the forces of denial and distraction, the hyper acceleration of time, and the collapse of space—make the labyrinth an especially relevant metaphor for today's world. They also help us understand why so many people feel that things are spiraling out of control. But none of this must allow us to lose sight of the fact that life was also bewildering in ancient Greece, otherwise we would not have been bequeathed the myth of the labyrinth. Despite the vast technological and social chasm that separates their world from ours, the inner challenges we face remain essentially unchanged. The hero's journey requires us to confront our fears—personal and collective. We face the Minotaur and the labyrinth, our own fears and limitations, society's ills, and all the rest of it. That was Theseus' challenge, and it remains yours and mine today.

ॐॐॐॐ

In today's shrunken and interdependent world, the impact of small-scale, private errors easily ripples out beyond the strictly local. Ecologists talk of the "butterfly effect": our world is so interconnected that when a butterfly flaps its wings in the Amazon, it can affect ecosystems as far away as Alaska or Antarctica. *Our* wrong choices can have a remote "butterfly effect," too. And of course these effects are compounded by the fact that there are now more than six billion of us on the planet.

The power of modern technology amplifies misguided choices in today's world for another reason, too. Our modern-day Minotaur is on steroids. Thanks to the wonders of chemistry, we can now store the murder of millions in a vial. Wrong decisions can produce horrific consequences like never before.

The net result is that today more than ever, we are living on the razor's edge. The visionary design scientist R. Buckminster Fuller believed that we have arrived at a moment in history when we have a choice between two starkly contrasting options: "utopia or oblivion." It is either create a world that works for all, or a world that works for none—and that could mean the extirpation of our species. Given the enormity of the stakes, it is absolutely imperative that we choose wisely. But can this be done if we are lost in our many labyrinths, where our judgment is by definition confused and distracted and ungrounded? Perhaps not. And so our first challenge must be to find our way into the light.

That is why I have written this book—to share two inter-linked conceptual frameworks, the "triad" and the "integral way," that can, I believe, help us find our way out of the personal and collective labyrinths that time and circumstance have mired us in. It is a "self-help" book in that it addresses the personal search for self, and a "world-help" book in that it offers a way to approach our great collective challenge. And although its being both these things may seem paradoxical, it actually isn't. In our massively intertwined world, the two have become one and the same.

The triad and the integral way are fully scalable: they can help us at the micro and macro levels, and also at levels in between. In addition to helping us better understand our own individual psyches and address our overarching cultural crisis, the triad and integral way can also provide insight into our interpersonal relations and the organizations we are involved in. It follows, therefore, that this book has been written for people who desire positive change at the personal, interpersonal, institutional, or cultural level.

This is also a book for people who are interested in leadership. The material presented in these pages is not only about understanding from an outsider's perspective how positive change can happen; it is also about integrating into one's being those special qualities of self that enable a person to help drive that change.

I have also written this book for the different voices that inhabit us. As we shall see, each of us contains three subpersonalities: a strategically oriented self, whom I call the "strategist," a socially oriented self (the "citizen"), and a meaning-oriented self (the "seeker"). I might plausibly have written this book for any of these three characters: it could have been a solution-centered book for the strategist, a book about our interpersonal relationships and civic responsibilities for the citizen, or an awakening-the-soul book for the seeker. As things have turned out, however, there is material in this book for all three subpersonalities. It is about strategy, dialogue, and identity in roughly equal measure. My impulse, in other words, has been integral.

I have also sought to be integral politically. I grew up surrounded by my parents' liberal friends, and I have spent much of my adult life among political progressives. It would have been easy for me to write this book for this audience, and to some extent I have—but only to some extent.

This was a deliberate decision. For some time, I have been convinced that if we are ever to emerge from our modern-day labyrinth, we must start reaching out to people whose beliefs and value systems feel alien to us. Progressives need to do this, and conservatives too. Outreach must be the first step, and from there we must find solutions that work for everyone. This book has been written for anyone, conservative or centrist or progressive, who finds merit in this view.

☙☙☙☙

If one is taking a tour, it is useful to know something about one's tour guide, so I will conclude this prologue with a few words about myself. I was trained as a lawyer, and after trying my hand at this and that, I turned my full attention to the environment and related issues during the late 1980s, where I have been working as a writer, entrepreneur, and consultant ever since.

For the most part I have specialized in business and what is variously known as "sustainable development" and "sustainability," a field of endeavor that can best be understood as the attempt to transform society from a place where economic growth is destroying the environment and driving a wedge between rich and poor into a place where environmental health, social justice, and economic prosperity are all balanced and accommodated. Many of the examples in this book are drawn from personal experience, which is one reason there are as many references as there are to the world of business and sustainable development. But I keep returning to the sustainability crisis for another reason, too. It is the lens through which I see our current predicament, and given how massively inclusive a concept sustainability is—it embraces pretty much the full panoply of social and environmental issues—I suspect it is as useful a lens as any.

The writer Paul Hawken has written that we are "beginning a mythic period of existence,"[2] and I agree. I understand this to mean that this is an age when the stakes are almost inconceivably high, and furthermore that this is an age that urgently requires heroes. Yet ours is a culture that induces sleepwalking, which is exactly the opposite of heroism. What will it take to awaken us out of our collective trance? Where is the thread that will guide us safely to the exit of our several labyrinths? What new identity does our time demand? These are the questions I take up in these pages.

PART 1:
Discovering The Triad

CHAPTER 1:
UNFINISHED BUSINESS

A Severed Conversation

On May 9, 1979, two men broke into my parents' modest ranch-style home in Bedford Hills, New York, entered their bedroom armed with a gun and a silencer, and killed them as they slept. From there, they went into the living room and helped themselves to a few drinks. They took a camera, a fur coat, a Japanese sword, and a few other items—maybe $1,000 worth in all—and departed, leaving the whisky bottles lying on the floor.

The following afternoon, I was coming to the end of another working day at McGraw-Hill in New York City when I received a telephone call from the National Humanities Center in North Carolina. My father, who was the founder and president of the organization, had been expected on a plane but hadn't arrived. Did I know what had happened? I did not, and set out to learn more.

A telephone call to the Bedford Hills police was not reassuring. There had been a double murder up the road, but the police had done a house-to-house check and there had been no other incidents. I asked them to revisit my parents' home.

After an endless two hours, the police called. My worst fears were realized: my parents had been murdered. I asked if a shotgun had been the weapon: somewhere in those past hours, I had picked up the rumor that the other two murders had been committed that way. They said no.

I didn't inquire further. "I'll be there as soon as I can."

A friend gave me and my wife of nine months a lift to Bedford Hills. As we drove through the twilight, grim scenarios raced through my mind. Rape. Ax murders. Torture. I readied myself for them all.

My parents' usually tranquil home was teeming with activity. Television cameras had been set up and spotlights penetrated the night. The police wouldn't allow me inside the house—the crime scene was off limits. I asked how my parents had died. They told me they had been murdered in their sleep, or close to that. After that long car ride filled with nightmare fantasies, this came as a relief.

What followed seemed relatively easy. I answered the police's questions as best I could. It seemed they had been killed the night before. If their time-of-death estimate was correct, my wife and I had been enjoying a drink at the Café de la Paix, just off Central Park, as they were being murdered.

We spent that night at the nearby home of a friend of my parents. Around two o'clock, I decided to try to sleep. I dozed off and, as dawn was breaking, awoke to birdsong and the view, immediately outside the window, of a tree in full bloom. For a moment I slipped out of human time. The birdsong was eternal, the tree eternal too. Millions upon millions of years had gone by, and nothing ever changed. How profoundly trivial human dramas like this were! The heart was like a curtain. Peel back our passion for life, strip away our desperate hunger for survival, and this was what remained. Beauty and indifference beyond imagining.

Early the next week, a memorial service was held at Columbia University, where my father had been teaching philosophy for forty years. The chapel was overflowing. A few years before, Wolfgang Friedmann, a professor at the law school, had been murdered by muggers on the street outside the School of International Affairs. Friedmann had survived Nazi Germany, and for him to have been brought down by a couple of street thugs had struck many people, including my father, as wildly unjust and absurd. Now the same fate had befallen my father. For many in the audience, it was like lightning striking twice.

Six weeks later, the killers were apprehended. They were middle-aged and looked like accountants. They were sentenced to four life terms, one for each murder, to be served consecu-

tively. One of them died of cancer in 1988. The other is impris-
oned in upstate New York. He comes up for parole in 2091.

ॐॐॐॐॐ

I didn't mourn my parents' death as fully as I might have. I
had several bouts of weeping during the first days, but I never
really purged myself completely. I'm not particularly good at
mourning: my impulse is to buck up and move on. I may have
gotten this trait from my father, who also preferred to focus on
the future. But there was more to it than that. Children's relationships with their parents are always complicated, and mine
was no exception. I loved my parents very much, yet at the time
of their death much remained unresolved in our relationship.
The reasons were both personal and cultural. My father was a
prominent spokesman for rationalism and liberal humanism.
He had a most impressive pedigree: he held an endowed chair at
Columbia, had received awards for being the best teacher at the
university, was the author of the influential and critically
acclaimed books *The Case for Modern Man* and *The Democratic
Prospect*, had served as Assistant Secretary of State for Educational and Cultural Affairs under Lyndon Johnson, was the
founder of the National Humanities Center, and more. When
William Bennett, the second-in-command at the National
Humanities Center under my father (and at the time a political
liberal), was asked by *The New York Times* to identify his three
leading role models, he named Gandhi, Ronald Reagan, and my
father—quite a combination!

This added another dimension to my youthful tussle for
individuation. Not only was I rebelling, like so many sons,
against my father, which would have been challenge enough; I
was also asserting myself against a man who for many people
embodied the best values of an entire culture.[3]

These difficulties were compounded by the fact that I came
of age during the 1960s. My father viewed as anathema much of
what I was donning as my new identity—my romantic embrace
of spontaneous emotion, my intellectual flirtation with radical
philosophers like Franz Fanon and Herbert Marcuse, my youth-

ful fascination with hippie free-love culture, and much more. I felt similarly about many of his positions, which struck me as short on the requisite emotional and moral fervor. My inarticulate intuitions annoyed him, his eloquent impatience annoyed me. Affection jostled with tension. Although we grew closer in the years before he died, there were still great silences between us. Then his death came, ending our incomplete conversation and the chance for resolution.

In another sense, however, the conversation continued, and it continues to this day. During my father's life, we had been talking at each other through the mists, and although he was gone now, the mists remained. If I was ever going to resolve this relationship to my satisfaction, I needed a language, and beyond that, a framework, that would define and illuminate who he was, and who I was, and the ways in which we were the same, and different. I needed something I could hold up to my father and say, "Look, this is who we are," and have him smile with understanding.

Close to two decades later, I received an unexpected gift. It was the framework I had been longing for without knowing I wanted it, and it emerged from my unconscious. I call it the triad, and it, together with a related framework I call the integral way, is the subject of this book.

Our New Challenge

Telling personal stories is always valuable, but I would not presume to tell this one if I were not convinced of its broader applicability. As a framework for understanding, the triad extends far beyond the strictly personal. Like ripples radiating out from a tossed pebble, its components make their way out into the world. The triad is what is known as a fractal, a term for a pattern that recurs at differing levels of organizational complexity. In nature, fractals shape such things as clouds, mountains, and coastlines. The triad is a fractal because its patterns underlie and animate human systems at every level of complexity from the intrapsychic up through the broader culture. Our psyches, our social relations, our institutions, our politics, and our cultural values are all shaped by the triad.

Thus this is not only a father-son story, by which I mean that it is not only about a father and his son, and not only a story. It is also a meditation on the subtle and complex relationship between self and society, on the conflicts that are tearing apart our institutions and our culture, and on how to go about addressing these challenges, both personally and collectively.

My father came of age during the 1930s. The specter haunting that decade was totalitarianism. His values—liberalism, reason, generosity of spirit—were their antidote.

Today we have a new demon knocking at the door: the sustainability crisis. Scientists tell us that within the next half-century, and quite possibly sooner, we may find ourselves inhabiting a planet with a dramatically weakened capacity to sustain life. It seems ecosystems have "buffer zones" that allow them to tolerate insults rather well—up to a point. But when the buffer overflows, the insults can no longer be absorbed, and what is known as "ecosystem collapse" occurs: the ecosystem's capacity to sustain life becomes vastly diminished. Everywhere on the planet, warning bells are going off that we are deep into the buffer zone and, in some cases, already beyond it.

Another grave and closely related danger is climate change, which, according to insurance-industry analysts, could bankrupt the global economy by mid-century and produce disasters and dislocations on a scale unprecedented in human history. Possibilities include Florida and Louisiana submerged by a sea rise occasioned by melting icecaps, and the still more nightmarish scenario of an average global temperature rise of over ten degrees Fahrenheit by 2100, devastating ecosystems everywhere.

Environmental quality is in precipitous decline, mostly due to the mutually reinforcing effects of three separate villains—pollution, overpopulation, and extreme poverty. Two-thirds of the world's population currently subsists on under $4 a day. Conditions like these drive people to desperate measures, including devastating the environment they, and we, all depend on. The gap between rich and poor is growing; everywhere, the social fabric is decaying. With communal trust in decline, more and more people must make their way on their own in what feels like an increasingly hostile world. This means making out as best they can, and to hell with everyone and everything else. In this way, the threat to the environment—our natural capital—is fed by our deteriorating social fabric—our declining social capital. And although these are the things we should be paying attention to, the twin horrors of war and terrorism have claimed center stage instead.

This is a grim set of problems indeed, and to make matters worse, it isn't immediately obvious who or what will make things better. There was a time when people counted on their governments to improve their lot, but that seems quite the long shot nowadays. It is the rare government that has the will, or even the imagination, to meet the current crisis. And while corporations have the money and muscle to address the challenge, they lack the motivation. Executives are under intense pressure to produce short-term profits, and so social and ecological issues get short shrift. Indeed, the gap between corporate proclamations of good intention and their actual performance is so wide that some observers have pronounced the so-called corporate social responsibility movement dead. And of course, the recent rash of corporate integrity scandals only lends credence to the view that global corporations are marquee villains in our current planetary drama.

As if all this were not enough, there is yet another cause for concern. Our usual approach to problem-solving is in failure mode, too. In the United States and other Western industrialized countries, we rely on the judicial model of decision-making. Advocates argue either side of a proposition and the process produces an outcome that favors one side, or the other, or splits the difference. In principle this works quite well, and in the past it has worked well in practice, too. It is, in fact, the essence of democracy.

But it is not working today. Disenchantment with democracy, or what passes for it these days, is widespread. The political process often seems like a charade. We are witnessing an ongoing riches-to-rags story: our democratic process, that shining gift to humanity from our Founding Fathers, has lost much of its glory and now comes across, all too often, as a shabby sham. Hamilton and Jefferson are down and out in America.

Underlying the failure of governance is a failure of perspective. We no longer make our decisions by thinking out the consequences of our actions over seven generations, as some Native American tribes are celebrated for doing. Seven days, or months, or, at the outside, years, is more like it. Catastrophes that may await us two or three or five decades down the road cannot sustain our attention, even if they are very likely to occur and demand immediate action. The result is an appalling lack of resolve and leadership—and an unremitting, rudderless drifting toward the abyss.

Along with the nuclear threat, the sustainability crisis is one of the two great dangers of the new century, the current furor over terrorism notwithstanding. My father's values, worthy as they are, are not up to the current challenge. Totalitarianism is not our main obstacle today; a mindset that remains largely oblivious to the grave danger posed by our deteriorating natural and social capital is. A philosopher might say that my father's values are necessary but not sufficient. We need new values—a new self-sense, really. The triad and the integral way provide guidance in this matter.

This is a personal story, then, and it is also a philosophical and political one. It is a story of the heart, and a book about conceptual frameworks, and a look at the state of our soul. And most of all, it is a call to action.

CHAPTER 2:
THE GEOGRAPHY OF THE TRIAD

Energies of the Gods

It was late one evening in March 1999, as I lay in bed drifting off to sleep, that it first occurred to me that people engage in essentially three types of relationship during their lives. They pursue goals, they engage with others and the natural world, and they try to make sense of the mystery of their existence.

Three types of relationship: with objectives, with what psychologists call the "other," and with meaning.

Over the months that followed, I found myself thinking more and more about the three realms—or the triad, as I came to call it. It became the lens through which I viewed the world. Time and again, I came home from a social gathering or movie and excitedly told Deborah, my wife of two years, how the model helped explain what I had just experienced. It became close to an obsession for me. By June 1999 I was wondering if there might be a book in this. The next month I started writing. I told friends it was like an alien birth: I hadn't planned on writing it, I didn't even want to write it, it just insisted on coming out.

Four months later I had completed a long and muddy first draft. Friends and colleagues provided feedback. They told me I had buried the story about my father and that it wanted to come out. Only then did I begin to understand why the triad had such projectile-like energy for me. I was birthing a framework that would render me articulate, that would end the long silence with my father.

Now, four years later, I have come to understand the triad in the following way. We begin with a concept I ascribe various names to over the course of this book—domains, realms, or dimensions. These domains can be thought of as force fields, each with its own intricate and idiosyncratic cluster of values and attitudes. When I close my eyes, I envision them as cosmic bodies pulsating with energy. They cannot be found in physical space, though, but in our inner world.

The domains are not made of atoms and molecules; they are constructed out of the complex set of emotions and aspirations that is awakened by our three primary types of relationship— with end goals, the other, and our subjective life-experience. The domains have been part of the human experience since time immemorial: they are universal psychological principles, a fact that makes it very difficult to resist according them an existence independent of our own mortal lives. More than half a century ago, the psychologist Carl Jung proposed that there was a collective unconscious, a storehouse where what he called the archetypes, universal symbols bearing deep meaning for humans, reside. Jung positioned the collective unconscious as being present inside all of us and also existing quasi-independently, by virtue of its timeless qualities. So it is with the three domains as well; they too have a life of their own. In fact, I suspect they may have come to me from the collective unconscious! The gods of the ancient pantheons are Jungian archetypes, and it pleases me sometimes to imagine the three domains as divine winds, blown into our souls from high atop Mount Olympus.

When we unpack the domains, what do we find? First of all, they contain different aptitudes, or what psychologists call *lines of development*. The objective domain houses our cognitive abilities, the social domain is where our interpersonal skills reside, and the depth dimension is home to our artistic and spiritual capacities. People tend to be more or less skilled in these areas. Jane has impressive analytical capabilities but is clumsy socially. Joe is a talented artist but seemingly incapable of analytical thinking. These aptitudes—these lines of development— are one of several patterns we find when we unpack the domains.

The domains also contain the three subpersonalities—the strategist, the citizen, and the seeker—each of which embodies the goals, values, and yearnings of the realm from which it springs. Each of these subpersonalities comes complete with its own worldview, which an Internet source called the Wikipedia defines as "more-or-less systematized sets of opinions on the structure of the universe, the meaning of life and one's relationship with society."[4] Basically, a worldview is a lens for interpreting the world. It is a useful construct, although I prefer the writer Robert Anton Wilson's synonym "reality tunnel," which reminds us that every worldview comes with walls as well as vistas. One of the main points of this book is that the strategist, the citizen, and the seeker all bring unique insights to the table—and they all wear blinders, too.

The three domains are created equal. They exist side-by-side, on the same level plane. But there is more to the matter than that. One of the core premises of this book is that there are higher, more inclusive levels of consciousness. Thus, while the domains inhabit a flat plane, they are best conceived of as plateaus on a journey that takes us up through higher and higher levels of psychological and spiritual growth.

When I initially conceived the triad, I assumed that no single domain was privileged over any other. This was a vision I had had, and the vision placed the domains on a single plane. Subsequently, however, I realized that there was a close overlap between the triad and aspects of a model of psychological development called Spiral Dynamics. Developed by the professor of psychology Clare Graves, the Spiral Dynamics framework proposes that we travel up a spiral of consciousness, both personally and collectively, from less to more evolved levels. According to Graves's model, there are two tiers of consciousness: the first has six levels and the second has two, making eight in all, and each level is identified by a particular worldview. It turns out that the triad's social domain, objective domain, and depth dimension bear striking resemblance to Graves's fourth, fifth, and sixth levels, respectively. And what I call the integral way, a reality tunnel that integrates the three domains at a higher level, smacks heavily of Graves's "second tier."

Now, what are we to make of this? Is the triad flat or is it hierarchical? The unlikely answer is both, and as it happens, the Spiral Dynamics model can help us understand how this can be so. The Spiral is unquestionably hierarchical—one ascends from level to level, and from the first to the second tier. But something important happens once one's psychological center of gravity has settled into the second tier. One comes to realize that none of its levels are privileged over any others, notwithstanding the Spiral's hierarchical structure. This is because each level contributes equally to our individual and collective journey up the Spiral. When it comes to Spiral Dynamics, you can have your hierarchy and eat it too.

And so it is with the triad as well. The domains are created equal, and they are also arranged hierarchically. Like the Spiral Dynamics framework, the triad is paradoxical.

As we get more deeply into the triad, we shall see that this is not at all surprising. The depth dimension, which is home to concepts like the collective unconscious and the triad, is also a sanctuary for the improbable and paradoxical. The rules down there differ from what we have grown accustomed to in our sunlit, ordered world.

A Philosophical Aside

Having identified what the triad is, let me hasten to add a few words about something it is not. The material in this book belongs to an emerging school of thought known as integral thinking. The leading articulator of this approach is the philosopher Ken Wilber, who proposes that we can understand how the world is structured by viewing it through a lens divided into four quadrants defined by axes of objective and subjective, individual and collective. If we look at the human experience through the lens of the four quadrants, one quadrant looks at the *objective aspects of the individual*, such as the neurophysiological aspects of the brain and organism; another looks at the *objective aspects of the collective*, such as the techno-economic mode of the society; another looks at the *subjective aspects of the collective*, such as the different values and assumptions of the culture; and the fourth quadrant looks at the *subjective aspects of the individual*, or the person's inner state of consciousness.

Wilber reduces these four to what he calls the "big three," consisting of the objective world, both individual and collective—"It"—plus the subjective individual—"I"—and subjective collective—"We." Wilber's framework is an ontology, a philosophical proposition about the nature and structure of reality.

I owe a sizable debt to Wilber, whose views have influenced me considerably. While readers who are familiar with his work will find resemblances between the triad and his big three, there are considerable differences too, not the least of which is that the triad does not purport to be what Wilber calls a "theory of everything." Rather than put forth a hypothesis about the nature of reality, I have limited myself to the more modest proposition that the triad is a structure of the self that we project onto our creations.

That said, it is also the case that I regularly discuss the domains as if they had an existence entirely independent of our mortal selves. On occasion I do this for dramatic effect, and more often because the universal and timeless quality of the domains leaves me with little choice but to accord them the same semiautonomous status as Jung's collective unconscious. It is almost as if the domains have a will of their own. They insist on being viewed this way.

The Triad

As we have seen, the triad proceeds from the premise that we engage in three basic types of relationship during our lives—with our goals, with other people and the natural world, and with our own subjective life-experience. It then proposes that we all have within us three distinct subpersonalities—the strategist, the citizen, and the seeker—whose function it is to manage these relationships.

The Strategist

The strategist's job is to get things done as quickly and accurately as possible. I call the strategist's home the "objective domain" because it is where we pursue our end goals (our objectives), and also because it is a way of being in the world that prizes objectivity (as distinguished from subjectivity)—clear thinking, clean data assessment, and the like. The strategist is a cognitive specialist.

There is a scalpel-like quality about the strategist. James Burke and Robert Ornstein call this the "axemaker's gift": "[I]n our ancient past the axemaker talent for performing the precise, sequential process that shaped axes would later give rise to the precise, sequential thought that would eventually generate language and logic and rules which would formalize and discipline thinking itself."⁵ The objective domain hosts our linear, strategic intelligence. The strategist who makes his or her home there gets us from here to there fast, faster, fastest. Strategists get things done, and they get them done efficiently.

When strategists are on their game, the experience is invigorating. These operations of mind, this single-minded focus on an end goal, this steadfast commitment to the sort of overview that leads to accelerated progress—all this creates a euphoria that is not unlike the feeling one gets from being on a mountaintop. The air is clear, the mind alert, the jungle with all its thickets and confusions far away. From this place where one feels almost able to touch the sky, complete knowledge seems possible and the opportunities seem endless.

The Citizen

The citizen is focused on engaging what psychologists call the "other," whether that be other people, their creations, or the world of nature. We are animals, and as animals we go out and encounter the world, everything from trees to fish to lions to pussycats to cars to buildings to art to other people. We stand in community with all these things and more, indeed with all nature.

Most of our encounters with the other are with other people. We are not only animals, we are also pack animals, and this produces a familiar set of emotions and behaviors. We yearn to belong to the group, and we fear being excluded. We have an impulse to nurture other members of our tribe, and sometimes to dominate them. We smile, laugh, share, and grieve together—and sometimes go on rampages, too. All these modes of relating are aspects of the citizen. And the space where it all occurs I call the "social domain."

But interacting with other people is not all we do as animals. We also live and die. Every encounter with the other contains unpleasant possibilities, up to and including sudden death. The citizen is the part of us that is charged with exercising the life-skills that enable us to successfully negotiate these encounters with the other. Strategists pursue survival strategies too, but theirs are more long-term—they require a pause for thought—and they also take place privately, inside one's own mind. Citizens, by contrast, operate at the interface where our private self engages the external world.

Despite my use of terms like "society," "social domain," and "citizen," we must always remember that the domain I am referring to includes the whole natural environment, which we, as animals, are also in relationship with. When we collapse this domain into human society, we do it, and more importantly, ourselves, a disservice. Yet it is also the case that in this book my primary focus vis-à-vis this domain is on our relationships with other people. And this is why I refer to this realm as "society" and the "social domain."

As for "citizen," I have chosen that term because the nature and extent of our civic responsibilities is one of this book's running themes. For many people, "citizen" is a heroic word, evoking patriotic images of flag and musket-bearing revolutionary-era soldiers. For others, it conjures up a naïve and facile self-sense that is badly out of step with our times. Both interpretations miss the mark, it seems to me. We need to update our understanding of citizenship so that it is accorded the dignity it warrants without requiring it also to be draped in images that have been appropriated by the political right. As I use the term in these pages, the citizen embodies that aspect of ourselves that steps out into the social domain and participates in the life of the community, shorn of both the sentimentalism of the right and the cynicism of the disaffected.

The Seeker

Last but not least, there is the seeker, who is preoccupied with probing the mystery of our existence. The seeker inhabits the "depth dimension," so named because that is where we must go—into our own depths—in the search for meaning.

I conceive of the depth dimension in an essentially Jungian sense, as the unconscious or the void. It is the source of art, the seat of the imagination, the forge of the stories we devise to infuse our life experience with meaning. It is where we engage the deep issues in life, things like our mortality and our relationship to the sacred. It is also where we encounter our deepest solitude, our darkest shames, and our most intense desires. And finally, it is where we experience our own authenticity. When asked by interviewer Bill Moyers about people's desire to know the meaning of life, the mythologist Joseph Campbell answered that it wasn't the *meaning* of life people were after so much as the *experience*. More than anywhere else, we discover this experience of living in the depth dimension.

All Jumbled Together

The strategist, the citizen, and the seeker claim space inside us like separate kingdoms or discrete political entities. They are fundamentally different ways of being in the world; it is almost as if we suffer from a case of multiple personality disorder.

The contrast between these three selves isn't usually all that evident, though. We bumble along with them more or less jumbled together and doing their different jobs as best they can. I chat on the phone with a friend I rarely see (the citizen), I give thought to how and where we might meet for dinner (the strategist), and I wonder vaguely if we'll get around to talking about the truly meaningful things in our lives (the seeker). The three selves do their work more or less simultaneously. They are all squeezed together, so to speak, on the same couch.

This is how things usually are. Sometimes, however, the domains disengage and it is suddenly revealed how deeply different they are. Such a moment occurred in the opening minutes of a conference I attended several years ago in Houston, when the facilitator invited the one-hundred-plus participants, who were seated at small round tables, to share their guiding life-principles with the others at their table. The moment we settled into our assignment, the mood in the room shifted palpably. It became deeper, slower, more viscous. The reason for this was apparent the moment I thought about it: we had switched spaces. We had been operating in society mode, functioning as social animals, feeling our way among strangers. The facilitator's request shifted us into the more soulful recesses of the depth dimension.

Like a Family

The strategist, the citizen, and the seeker are like children in a family. Sometimes they quarrel, sometimes they get along. This can be a problem in its own right, and all too often each of us, the "parent," makes things worse by playing favorites. We identify with one domain and scorn one or both of the others. Beth, a depth-dimension artist, holds Bill, an objective-domain lawyer, in disdain because he's too "straight" and "soulless." Jane, a society-centered conservative who believes people's first duty should be to obey the rules of the social order, has no tolerance for Joe and his unconventional, disruptive, depth-dimension ways. And so on.

These conflicts happen all the time—so much so, in fact, that the dynamic has been immortalized in a fairy tale, those incomparable myths where our most basic patterns of behavior are recorded. We are all familiar with Cinderella, the story of a beautiful young woman who is neglected and abused while her two sisters are favored. This can be understood as a triad psychodrama. Cinderella lives in the depth dimension, which is where we find our authenticity. In rejecting her, Cinderella's sisters are rejecting their own authentic nature. It is only by raising Cinderella up, as her princely suitor does, that a healthy balance is restored.

This dynamic, in which the depth dimension is oppressed by the other domains, is a kingpin pattern in our culture. I call it the "tyranny of the objective."

A Longing for Harmony

Even as the strategist, citizen, and seeker are jockeying for position inside our psyches, we are also longing for something quite different. It is in our nature to crave harmony, equality, and balance among these three aspects of self.

When quarrels among the strategist, citizen, and seeker keep a dynamic balance from prevailing, we suffer in our hearts. This suffering is often unconscious—we are masters at adapting to circumstances, and we habitually accept dysfunctionality and imbalance as the norm. Yet even as we settle into our misalignments, we simultaneously retain a deep yearning for balance, for harmony. We never completely turn our backs on our longing for the sublime. We dream of utopian societies. We melt before exquisite art.

We are, in short, riddled by conflict. We play favorites, and we long to harmonize the realms. We impose the will of the strategist on the citizen, or the citizen on the seeker, through a sort of intrapsychic *force majeure*, and we long for an internal governance system that is a true democracy. We yearn for our fairy tale to have a happy ending.

A Fractal Pattern

The strategist, the citizen and the seeker are "deep structures" of the self. They shape our psyches at a largely unconscious level, and we then project that patterning into much of what we invest with psychic energy. The triad is thus a template we use to construct our created world. Our interior and interpersonal lives, and also our institutions and culture, are stamped with the imprint of the triad.

For instance, when prejudices and quarrels among the strategist, citizen, and seeker happen inside individual psyches, they're called "neuroses." When they set people against each other, they're called "personality conflicts." When they happen at the broader cultural level, it's called "politics."

The Henry Higgins Fallacy

Not only does the triad define our created world, it also determines, in significant measure, the extent to which we are happy, if by that we mean being largely free of neurosis and dysfunctionality. When the strategist, the citizen, and the seeker are interacting as equals—when they are balanced and in harmony—we are happy. When they are not, we are not.

This seems simple enough, but unfortunately we often support repression and imbalance through our ignorance. In one recurrent pattern, we side with one subpersonality and wish the others would simply go away, instead of working to have everyone get along. The seeker desires the exclusive companionship of seekers, the strategist of strategists, and so on. I call this the "Henry Higgins fallacy," after the character in the musical comedy *My Fair Lady* who laments, "Why can't a woman be like me?"

Even if we don't impose this utopian and doomed fantasy on our psyches, so long as we allow these subpersonalities to persist in their unruly jostling for positioning, we are left feeling trapped, confused, and frustrated—and because the sources of our discontent remain unknown to us, we cannot find a way out of our predicament.

This defines the essence of the labyrinth—confusion and a sense of overwhelm at the prospect of ever finding one's way out—and it is a labyrinth with a fractal nature, like the triad from which it springs: it recurs at levels ranging from the private and personal through the interpersonal and institutional to the broadly cultural and political.

A few examples may be useful. I now believe that my conflict with my father resulted from the fact that we favored different domains. He identified with the objective domain and its commitment to linear reason, while I, a product of the sixties, was an unabashed advocate of the depth dimension. His strategist had no tolerance for my seeker, and vice-versa. And since we didn't have a framework for discussing our differences, we were left with unresolved tension.

Another example: a friend of mine has a strong mystical streak and is also quite fun-loving and gregarious. Usually these two aspects of himself, his seeker and his citizen, get along quite well. Occasionally, though, his inward-turning seeker gets annoyed with all that playfulness, which feels like a distraction from the seeker's more earnest and eternal pursuits, and he demands that his citizen self make himself scarce. When that happens, my friend becomes withdrawn to the point of seeming inhospitable. But his antipathy is not really directed toward his friends: it is his own citizen, that antic, social self of his, that he is denying.

Institutional disagreements often stem from these "realm wars," too. Several years ago, I participated in a day-long strategy retreat that had been organized by a Boston-based nonprofit I was working with. About twenty-five people representing a broad variety of backgrounds and constituencies participated. Among them were two well-known advocates for voluntary simplicity, a movement that encourages people to dramatically reduce their consumption. A prominent sociologist spoke for the black community, which is concerned most of all with *in*voluntary simplicity. Assorted media specialists and business executives were there, too.

The topic was, How do you get people in the mainstream to embrace sustainability? It soon became apparent that people differed on the answer to a degree that had them frowning at each other's observations.

I watched these displays of irritation with increasing concern. If putative allies kept getting under each other's skin over theoretical questions like this, what did that say for our ability to work together? The session concluded with that persnickety edge still there—and now I, too, was grimacing in frustration. This had been a wonderful opportunity to build consensus and to lay the foundation for a focused strategy. Instead there had only been wheel-spinning, with no real progress made.

It was not until later that I realized why things had gone wrong. Realm wars had created that low buzz of annoyance.

Three models of change were being advocated by the participants. One was the *business* model of change, and predictably it was the corporate types—the strategists—who were arguing for it. The crux of their argument was: show me the money. Explain the matter rationally and appeal to people's self-interest. Make the sale to their left brain.

The media specialists had taken a different tack. They were arguing for building public awareness, for getting people who were sympathetic to sustainability elected to public office. Their brief was society.

The voluntary simplicity advocates had been arguing for what I found myself thinking of as the "conversion" or "missionary" model of change. They didn't believe you could get people to embrace sustainability by appealing to reason. Sustainability was a creed, a gospel. The only way to "get" it was at the gut level. They were speaking for, and from, the depth dimension.

At the meeting we'd gotten stuck, as partisans of the three domains went back and forth making their case. We hadn't had a failure of process so much as of insight. If we had better understood the biases that had produced the irritation in the room, we might have been able to rise above them.

Conflict and dysfunctionality are pervasive in our psyches, in our interpersonal relations, in our institutions, and in our broader culture, too. Collectively they create our labyrinth—

and they are often the result of unresolved and ill-understood disputes between the strategist, the citizen, and the seeker.

The Integral Way

If the triad provides insight into who we are and how we go wrong, the integral way offers guidance on what we can do about it. Or, to put it another way, the triad tells us how we get trapped in the labyrinth, and the integral way shows us how to get out.

The integral way is how we manage this congeries of subpersonalities maturely and effectively. It is a process for achieving consensus and harmony, and for doing so in the many dimensions—intrapsychic, interpersonal, institutional, and cultural—where the triad makes its mark on the world. Imagine three horses harnessed to a coach: these are the three subpersonalities. If the coachman cannot control these steeds, he or she is helpless. We practice the integral way when we effectively manage the team. The self controls the subpersonalities, not the other way around.

Stripped to its essence, the integral way is a way to hold information, especially information about values and emotions. This information can come directly from our own depth dimension ("I feel happy this morning!") or it can come from another person or some other aspect of the social domain ("that person's values trouble me"). In either case, the inputs are mediated by the self, which has a double assignment relative to this information: it must note and then respond to it. Depending on who we are, we will note more or less information, and we will note it more or less accurately.

The integral way is a habit of mind. More specifically, it is a habitual way of noting and responding to information that is committed to noting more inputs rather than less, and to responding with a bias toward nonjudgment. It favors nonrejection, affirmation, inclusivity. Indeed, this is an essential feature of the integral way: a strong, if not quite absolute, commitment to inclusivity.

In this regard, the integral way resembles meditation, which teaches people to watch their thoughts and feelings without judgment. But meditation and the integral way are not at all the same. For one thing, meditation is an exclusively depth dimension practice. Its exclusive focus is on personal and spiritual growth. The integral way, as we shall see, has a secular as well as a spiritual dimension. In addition, meditation is generally deemed to require a formal practice. This is not the case for the integral way, which doesn't require that sort of commitment.

If we are using the triad as our framework, the commitment to inclusivity translates into not playing favorites with any of the three subpersonalities; the strategist, the citizen, and the seeker all get equal treatment.

When inclusivity is practiced over time, our perspective evolves, and in time this coalesces into a new, higher-level pattern of organization. We "transcend and include," in the words of Ken Wilber. This is the second essential feature of the integral way: the emergence of a new pattern of organization.

This process can roll out under the auspices of either the objective domain, the social domain, or the depth dimension. When it is engaged from the objective domain, its function is *strategic*: the integral way becomes a tool, a technique, a protocol for generating a desired outcome. Because the integral way has us working with an expanded set of inputs—more rather than less, "yes" rather than "no"—the answers we come up with are frequently quite different from what we might have thought of otherwise. For this reason, the integral way can be used as a technique for coming up with breakthrough solutions.

Under the auspices of the social domain, the integral way becomes a *framework for dialogue*. For instance, I can imagine its having been the basis for reconciling with my father. In my mind's eye, I see us sitting in front of a crackling fire, shifting triad concepts about in our minds and conversation as we once maneuvered pieces on the chessboard, and arriving at new understandings this way.

The integral way can also be applied in institutional and community settings, as I imagine could have been done to resolve the tension at the strategic-planning meeting I attended in Boston. Finally, it can be used as a framework for interior dialogue—my strategist in conversation with my seeker, and so on.

As an activity of the depth dimension, the role of the integral way is both *psychological* and *spiritual*. It is a process for shaping identity that when practiced over time can lead to the emergence of another discrete subpersonality, which I call the "sage." It is a fundamentally new self-sense, a new and higher-level pattern of organization that is unlike the strategist, citizen, and seeker in that it "transcends and includes" the other three. The sage possesses a perspective that unites the triple wisdom of the objective domain, the social domain, and the depth dimension into a more inclusive, higher-level whole. I suspect that this view of things is what the truly great spiritual teachers had in mind, although their teachings often get lost in translation and reduced to the immensely valuable but fundamentally different—and less than integral—insights of the depth dimension.

The Hero's Journey

As noted earlier, underlying this book is the assumption that there is a psychological ladder of development we travel up, both individually and culturally. We evolve from our identification with the strategist, citizen, or seeker to an identification with the sage, a self that includes and transcends all three.

There is a road map for this. It is called the hero's journey, and it is one of the timeless themes of myth. Essentially, it tells of a call to adventure; of a quest and challenges confronted; of a dark night of the soul, when all seems hopeless; and of metaphoric death and resurrection, at which point the journey begins anew. Often a wasteland is involved; the land has gone barren and the hero's challenge is to make it fertile again.

If you are familiar with the hero's journey, it is probably

thanks to the mythologist Joseph Campbell, who brought the narrative into the public eye with his book, *The Hero with a Thousand Faces*, and his subsequent *The Power of Myth*, a six-part public television documentary series with Bill Moyers that is the most popular PBS program of all time.

The triad provides a lens onto the hero's journey. He or she (and in our patriarchal mythical traditions it is usually a he!) is a member of the community, sometimes a prince and sometimes of royal character but not socially privileged. An objective-domain problem confronts the community: a dragon must be slain or a wasteland redeemed. Our hero steps forward.

Although the myth casts the problem as something external, the challenge is actually psychological. The dragon is an internal dragon or perhaps a Minotaur. The wasteland is an internal wasteland or labyrinth. The hero must confront and overcome a deep fear. Until that happens, he or she will not be whole. And that—wholeness, integration—is the goal.

But how is our hero to do this? There is only one way—by journeying into the depth dimension to confront the "shadow," where all he or she is most afraid of hides. This is the story of Orpheus traveling into Hades, and of Christ's harrowing of hell, and it is also the story of Theseus in the labyrinth.

It takes great courage to do this, but the prize is great, too. It makes the hero spiritually rich. By saying yes to something he previously rejected, the hero becomes more whole and undivided.

The last sequence in the hero's journey comes when the hero returns to society and places his or her hard-won treasure at the disposal of the community. Thus the hero comes full circle—but it isn't full circle, really, it's full spiral, for when the hero returns to society, he is a very different person from the one who left. He has integrated depth-dimension material, and this has made him stronger.

The hero's journey is a saga each of us reenacts over and over again—or fails to, by failing to confront our fear. We never become completely whole. The depth dimension is bottomless:

there is always more depth-dimension material to integrate. And so we never arrive at our destination. We never truly become sages. We are always sages-in-progress, always on the way.

Although our wisdom is never absolute, in relative terms the sage does provide wise counsel. The strategist, the citizen, and the seeker get lost in the labyrinth because their reality tunnels are too narrow. Not the sage, whose perspective integrates all three. The sage honors all three voices; he or she practices what I call "right balance"—the art of bringing each voice into play at the appropriate time.

Sages have another strength as well. They have successfully integrated their hero, by which I mean integrated into their bodies and beings the understanding that no one but ourselves can confront the Minotaur that lives inside each of us—and that only by engaging our world heroically can we forge a world that offers hope to future generations. The early-twentieth-century environmentalist Gifford Pinchot wrote: "The vast possibilities of our great future will become realities only if we make ourselves responsible for that future." The sage understands the truth of this.

CHAPTER 3:
THE THREE DOMAINS

The Objective Domain (the Strategist)

It is a million years ago. A hominid ancestor is eyeing a sharp stone that he has been using as a cutting tool. Its effectiveness is limited, though, and using it bruises his hand. Nearby lies a thick stick. The hominid stares at the stone, then at the stick, then back at the stone. A gleam comes into his eye. He takes a vine and ties stick and stone together. Presto! An axe! Our hirsute friend has engaged the objective domain, for what he has done is identify a problem—dimly, to be sure, but identified it—and a goal—remedy the problem—and then figured out how to do precisely that. The objective domain is first and foremost a *problem-solving* domain. It is all about end goals and strategies for getting there. It is analytical and diagnostic. Think "mental operations" and you are thinking of the strategist.

In a sense the objective domain is navigational. It addresses the question, *How do we get from here to there?*, and it does so across an endless range of subjects. The challenge at hand may be technological (*How do we make sharp tools? File stones into flints.*). It may be commercial (*How do we increase our profits by 10 percent next year? Invest more in marketing and advertising.*). It may be instructional (*How do we get people to think long-term and very long-term? Propose adding a zero to our calendar, 02002 instead of 2002, as the writer Stewart Brand has done.*).

The objective domain is predictive as well as navigational. *"If I charge that battlement, then I will die. If I stay here and lob flaming arrows over the ramparts, then my chances of survival are better."* Here, of course, predictive *is* navigational: our warrior's strategizing counsels him on how to get from the "here" of the battlefield to the "there" of being alive tomorrow.

The strategist is thus *future*-focused. Strategists are always trying to figure out how to get *there*, and "there" lies in the future. They've got tomorrow on their mind.

Predictive, "if-then" structures belong to the objective domain. Legal and ethical codes, for instance. *"If you commit theft, then your hand shall be cut off." "If you commit adultery, then God will punish you."* "If...then" defines a logical sequence, a path from cause to effect, and this linear, orderly process characterizes the objective domain. Isaac Newton conceived a cause-effect universe, billiard balls clicking together one after the other. This is how the strategist's mind works, moving logically and inexorably toward its final destination. It is a train chugging along to the tune of "if-then," the axe we use to hew a path through the jungle of choices the world throws our way.

Linear, left-brained, means/end, strategic, deterministic, and *instrumental reasoning* are terms we use to describe this style.

And it *is* a style, a way of being in the world. The strategist has a personality all his own. He is active, not passive. He does not surrender, he moves forward. And while both men and women can identify with and operate from the strategist, at the archetypal level he is masculine—"yang." He controls. (Come to think of it, the close relationship between the navigational impulse and masculine energy may be why so many men shy away from asking directions. Maybe they experience having to rely on someone else to get them "from here to there" as an affront to their masculine dignity.)

Powerful emotions are associated with the objective domain. The will to *achieve* is what drives us to get from "here to there." Whatever his specific goal may be, it is figuratively a mountain the strategist is climbing, and once he has made it to the top it feels like victory: we speak of "conquering mountains" and this is one reason why. So it is with all our goals: we overcome our obstacles, we prevail, we "conquer." And the view from the mountaintop—even the *prospect* of the view from the mountaintop—is bracing.

There is nothing intrinsically wrong with this emotion—it

is a necessary and invaluable aspect of human experience—but there is always the danger that it will spiral out of control. When our goal is to gain power over other people, or when we pursue our objectives without adequately considering the likely consequences—as was the case, many say, with the Manhattan Project—this drive can do enormous harm. Analytical, focused on achievement and conquest—these are all qualities of the archetypally masculine strategist.

The objective domain is Cartesian as well as Newtonian. By this, I mean that it functions by separating—mind from matter, self from other, subject from object. It is dualistic.

It is also reductionistic: it solves problems by making things small, by reducing things to their component parts. Inside the objective domain, the observer swells and the thing observed shrinks. The self becomes "bigger than it." There is a practical reason for this. Unless a problem is smaller than you are, it will overwhelm you psychologically. And so the first thing the strategist does in addressing a problem is shrink it down to size.

Written language emerges from the objective domain. Not only does it enhance the power to communicate, and as a result help solve problems, it also reduces what we experience to tiny letters, strung together one after the other. Remember those billiard balls? Alphabetic text turns the world into a linear chain and makes us, the observers, "bigger than it." There are profound differences between alphabetically literate and oral cultures, as Marshall McLuhan, Leonard Shlain and others have noted. This is because they are centered in the objective domain and the depth dimension, respectively.

The objective domain has many faces. It is the dictator plotting to eliminate his rivals and the mother agonizing over how to cure her baby. It is the scientist constructing an experiment to test a pet hypothesis, and the corporate executive strategizing how to meet the next quarter's profit targets. It is me at my desk at this very moment, trying to figure out what I am trying to say and how best to say it.

At its worst, the objective domain is ruthless and heartless.

At its best, it makes the world a better place and is wildly creative and great fun. Whatever its purpose, the same basic question drives it: *How do I get from here to there?* The objective domain is narrowed eyes and a racing mind. Spiritual teachers advise us to "be here now." The objective domain counsels something different: "Get there fast." And shows us how to do it.

The Voice of the Objective Domain

"Science is an integral part of culture. It's not this foreign thing, done by an arcane priesthood. It's one of the glories of the human intellctual tradition." –Stephen Jay Gould

"Whatever creativity is, it is in part a solution to a problem." –Brian Aldiss

"I love the smell of napalm in the morning. It smells like...*victory!*" –Robert Duvall as Colonel Kilgore in *Apocalypse Now*

The Social Domain (the Citizen)

Unlike the objective and depth domains, which are entirely interior, the social domain takes us out of ourselves, into relationship with what psychologists call the "other."

But let's first explore what the "other" is. Precisely what is it we are relating with? The answer is, all of nature, a category that includes people, who are, after all, part of nature. The social domain is where life encounters life. I, who was born and will die, meet you, who were born and will die. It is no different if I take a walk through a forest: the human life-form called "Carl" is encountering the life-form we call "trees."

This domain is thus home to physical nature, with the emphasis on the "physical." It is not the world as idea, not the world as repository for projected fantasies and emotions (that imagined world inhabits the depth dimension), but the world as actual physical stuff, atom and molecules and matter and life. It is mountains and forests and oceans, and the web of life in magnificently intricate interaction. And the world of human society, too. We are animals, and as animals we stand in relationship with the natural world and other human animals.

But it is not only what we ordinarily think of as "life" that we encounter in the social domain. There is also the vast universe of human artifacts. Our great genius as a species lies in our ability to make stuff. Some of it is beautiful (Mozart's music), some of it functional (row housing), some of it horrific (killing weapons), and some of it is junk (one hardly knows where to begin). The stuff we make is everywhere; both literally and figuratively, we spend our lives moving through it. When we visit a city, we walk by people on the street and we look up at the buildings. They are both part of our social world. When we go shopping, we pack our cart with consumables, pay the check-out clerk, load our car with what we've bought, and go home. Cart, consumables, check-out clerk, car—they're all part of the "other" we've encountered. And it is an "other," one might add, substantially devoid of nature.

These three things—nature, people, and the many physical artifacts people make—are what you encounter in the social domain.

Now that we've learned what we encounter in the social domain, let's proceed to the next question: what can people expect to get out of their encounter with it? (And please bear in mind that I am focusing on our social, tribal relations here, not on our relationship with physical nature.) You get, more than anything else, a sense of membership. Of *belonging*. For the ancient Greeks, being exiled from society was viewed quite literally as a fate worth than death. It led to death, inevitably, for one was no longer protected by the tribe, but it was a death without companionship or pride, and nothing could be worse.

What comes with belonging? To begin with, a sense of identity. In rigidly stratified societies, our caste tells us who we are. I am a Brahmin or an Untouchable. In more fluid, modern societies, we learn who we are from more subtle cues, which we increasingly get from advertising. We learn that it's good to be thin or get good grades or drink beer.

None of this is our authentic self, of course. It's our social identity, the persona we adopt to win favor. It's sometimes called a "false self" but that's a bit unfair. It's our *social* self, not our false self, and these are two distinct things.

We get something else from society as well. We get nurtured. As the Greeks knew, society is our main source of mutual protection. "We all need someone you can lean on," sing the Rolling Stones, while the poet Louis MacNeice invites us to *"Come then all of you, come closer, form a circle/Join hands and make believe that joined/Hands will keep away the wolves of water/Who howl along our coast. And be it assumed/that no one hears them among the talk and laughter."* The social domain provides physical and psychological security.

We pay a price for this security, though. The social structures of society are tribal, and this means, among other things, pecking orders, power structures, and unnecessary wars. If the objective domain is where we create conceptual hierarchies ("A is a better strategy than B"), society is where we create social ones ("C is entitled to more privileges than D"). It is where power relations are embedded and played out, where alpha males do their testosterone-charged thing. Thus society is "androgynous"—masculine in its support of hierarchy, feminine in its capacity to nurture. And it is also the home of authority—who's up, who's down—and of tradition, which underwrites the rules. Tradition and authority are core values here.

Some people celebrate, even idealize, society. Typically these are conservatives who speak reverently of things like law-and-order and the flag, and bemoan the loss of social cohesion and the decline in "family values." These people tend to venerate the past because that is where tradition and authority, which hold their world together, come from. Where the strategist is future-oriented, the citizen looks to the past.

As much as some people admire society, others are put off by it. These are the people who welcome change more than they resist it, who believe in themselves and the future more than in their fathers and the past. When these people contemplate society, they see a value system that suppresses personal freedom and supports social injustice. They are iconoclasts for whom the idols of tradition and authority exist mainly to be broken.

Anarchists take this one step further. They would like to see all the structures of society dismantled so that our depth-dimension selves could call the shots completely. This can't happen, of course. Society is here to stay. The domain isn't intrinsically good or bad; it simply *is*, like the other two domains.

༺༺༺༺༺

Now that we know what the "other" consists of and what we can expect from the social domain, let's ask one final question: what can society expect from us? (It is a two-way relationship, after all.) The answer is, society gets what we have to give, neither more nor less. But that only partly says it, for many people have wonderful things to contribute but never quite manage to offer it to society. Something, a sort of stage-fright, keeps them from transforming their private genius into a public gift.

And so we can also think of society as a stage. Our private lives play out in the objective domain (as mental activity) and the depth dimension (as soulful activity). The "stage" is where this internal activity coalesces into action—it is where we "show up," or don't. The indecisive Hamlet was strong in his mind and soul, but he faltered on the stage, which is where character translates into action. It is where our hopes and fears and bright ideas are made manifest in the world.

This, in turn, suggests something else. In science, a "field" is a place where something happens. Society is in this sense a "field," because it is where the objective domain and the depth dimension interact. Our objective goals and depth dimension souls weave a tapestry of self that is manifested in the social domain.

There is a scientific correlative to this. The objective domain, as noted earlier, is Newtonian—predictable, deterministic, and dominated by linear notions of cause-and-effect. The depth dimension is much more quantum in its basic nature. Randomness and indeterminacy are among its governing principles. Society is the "field" where the intrapsychic dance between Newtonian and quantum realities—between the determinate and the indeterminate, the orderly and the random—is played out. There is even a word for this sort of interaction: *stochastic*. The objective domain is Newtonian, the depth dimension is quantum, society is stochastic. It is where the dialectic between the objective domain and the depth dimension finds physical expression in the world.

To sum up, then, the social domain has four related but distinct identities. It is the "other," nature and people and all the artifacts people create. It is human society, with its many rules and rewards and tilt toward tradition and authority. It is the "stage," understood in the sense of how we show up in the world. And finally, it is a "field," that is, the place inside our psyches where the interactions between the objective domain and the depth dimension are transformed into behavior.

The Voice of Society

"Wealth among the Dagara [the author's tribe of origin] is determined not by how many things you have, but by how many people you have around you." –Malidoma Patrice Somé

"There is only one thing in the world worse that being talked about, and that is not being talked about." –Oscar Wilde

"In the beginning was the deed." –Johann Wolfgang Goethe

The Depth Dimension (the Seeker)

"Where do we come from, what are we, where are we going to?" asked the painter Paul Gauguin. All of us need meaning, context, a solid sense of self. The depth dimension is where the seeker goes to find these things. It is not a physical place so much as a void that we access with our imagination. Close your eyes and you will see thoughts, images, awarenesses, bubbling up in the space behind your eyes. This space, this black hole of potentiality, is the depth dimension.

In my office, I have an ink-wash by a friend, the artist Eugene Gregan. It portrays a man, an idealized figure from out of the imagination. His lids are lowered: he is either looking down or his eyes are closed. In his outstretched hand, he is grasping a low tree that he has just plucked from the earth. Its roots are plainly visible. The tree is bathed in yellow-golden light. He stands there holding it, eyes averted. For me, this captures the essence of our relationship with the depth dimension. The seeker reaches a blind hand into the darkness and emerges with burnished gold.

The gold of Gregan's image is the gold of meaning, the compass that gives structure and purpose to our lives. It is what the cultural historian Thomas Berry calls the "story." The depth dimension is where we go prospecting; the story is the gold.

We can also think of the depth dimension as a darkroom. We go into it and emerge with unlikely images—and sometimes we don't even emerge with images, but with our souls transformed instead.

If there is one overarching purpose to the depth dimension, as there is to the objective domain (prevailing) and the social domain (belonging), it is this: "becoming one." This has, of course, a double meaning. It means becoming fully separate, fully individuated—fully "oneself"—and it also means having the boundaries between self and other completely dissolve, that is, becoming "one with everything." As the Buddhist said to the hot-dog vendor, "Please make me one with everything."

This is paradoxical, of course. How can the depth dimension both shore up boundaries and tear them down? But this need not surprise us. "Either/or" thinking is objective-domain thinking. In the depth dimension, the rules are different. There, paradox isn't paradoxical. It makes perfect sense.

The depth dimension is ultimately unknowable, but it wears many masks: it is by far the most complex and multifaceted of the three domains. In addition to being where our seeker goes searching for meaning, it submits to the following interpretations, too:

- The wellspring of animal and transcendent passion;
- The "source"—the generative principle, the primordial mystery—and, as such, the seat of our spirituality;
- Where magic happens;
- The unconscious and the "shadow";
- The mythic imagination;
- Home of secrets and "the wound";
- The home of freedom;
- A "lunar," feminine place;
- Where we connect with our authentic self; and
- Where we experience our participation in the web of nature.

It is understandable if this seems like an unlikely number of aspects for a single domain. The answer to this lies in the fact that the void is an experience we can explain only by interpreting it, and interpretation is by definition a plural—and, more to the point, pluralistic—form. Given that the human imagination has been breathing meaning into the void for millennia, it is hardly surprising for it to have acquired as many dimensions as it has.

The Wellspring of Animal and Transcendent Passion

One way to understand the depth dimension is as what

remains when you strip away the mental constructs of the objective domain and the conventions of society. Who are we, really, once our mental operations and social habits are peeled away? People have been pondering this question for millennia and the answers fall into two basic camps, which we can characterize broadly as "materialist" and "mystical."

Materialists say that when push comes to grunt, we're beasts. Strip away mind and manners and you're left with our base animal nature—the appetite unleashed, id raw and unpolluted. Peel back civilization's veneer and you are left with brute uninhibited nature, the procreative instinct run amok.

An Italian film from the 1980s called *Devil in the Flesh* portrayed the depth dimension that way. In the movie, a terrorist gang is brought to trial. They are held in a cage inside the courtroom, where they are surrounded by *carabinieri* (the Italian military corps) and judged, from a high dais, by men in robes. Two of the prisoners, a man and a woman, start having sex—"making love" would be far too genteel a description. It is an intentionally mindless yet political statement—animal energy as a more authentic way of being. The *carabinieri* rush in, pandemonium breaks loose, the good bourgeois are badly shaken. There you have it, the drama made visible: the depth dimension, asserting itself boldly from within the confines of law (the objective domain) and authority (society). Freedom in fucking!

The more mystically inclined see things differently. They say that when we stop identifying with our thoughts (the objective domain) and our bodies (society), we find that what we really are is embodiments of God. *Maya*, illusion, peels away and we experience the One behind the Many, the Formlessness behind the Form. The depth dimension takes us not into the primal jungle, but into the mystic void.[6]

The Seat of Our Spirituality

The depth dimension is thus where the seeker goes to experience the divine. Allah, Jahweh, and God all live in the depth dimension, and what our prophets and messiahs do is journey there, encounter the divine, and return to society with the revealed Word, which is then packaged as Islam, Judaism, Christianity, or whatever. Organized religions are branded versions of the depth-dimension encounter with the divine.

Many of the qualities we associate with the divine reside in the depth dimension. The generative principle, to take just one example. In all the great creation stories, form emerges out of no-form, out of chaos. Today chaos is commonly understood to mean disorder, but that is a bit of a bad rap. Three thousand years ago, when the term was first used, it meant the source of all creation. Chaos was seen as life-giving and good, not entropic and anarchic. And chaos, understood in this positive sense as the source of all form and creativity, lives in the depth dimension.

Another term that is often associated with the divine is the "primordial mystery." God can never be completely known, theologians tell us. The same can be said for the depth dimension. No matter how much gold we mine, there is always more to be found. No matter how deeply you plumb the depth dimension, you can always go deeper. It has no end point, no bottom. The mystery remains.

In today's world we tend to be uncomfortable with this. "Mystery is a great embarrassment to the modern mind," the novelist Flannery O'Connor said.[7] This is because the modern mind is an objective mind, and the mystery inhabits the depth dimension. From the vantage point of the objective domain, it seems obvious that if we keep doing our science long enough, we will eventually crack all nature's codes. This view turns a blind eye to the irreducible mystery (divine or otherwise). But it is to be expected, given our dominant culture's need to be "bigger than it" and its wholesale rejection of the depth dimension.

This bias also explains why "chaos" has acquired a negative connotation. It is to be expected from a culture that operates under the tyranny of the objective domain, with its partiality for order.

The depth dimension has yet another affinity with the divine. It is where time slows down. Stops, even. If the objective domain shows us how to "get there fast," the depth dimension teaches us how to "get there slow"—or, in guru-speak, to "be here now," which is essentially the same thing. Most of us have probably experienced timelessness: we are making love, or meditating, and suddenly we slip into what feels like an eternal state. The more we are fully present—the more, that is, that we stop distracting ourselves with thoughts of past and future—the more we feel as if we are penetrating into the heart of time. It is a process that takes us down into the depth dimension. And as any serious meditator will tell you, the further down the journey takes us, the closer we come to experiencing the divine.

The depth dimension is thus where our time-sense is present-focused, compared with the future-oriented objective and past-centered social domains.

Let's pause here and interject a question: how can God be in only one domain? Are we to assume that the social and objective domains are somehow devoid of His presence? The answer to this is no, they are not—and to explain why this is so, we must understand the depth dimension's unique double nature. At one level, it is simply one of three domains that we can imagine lying aligned along a flat plane. Unlike the objective and social domains, however, the depth dimension has, well, *depth*. And not only does it have depth, but this depth is not limited to a single vertical silo. The depth dimension is a substrate. It underlies all three domains and endows them with a single coherent identity.

Imagine an eagle's-eye view of a landscape: two villages, and a place in the country, equidistant from the two, where a stream bubbles up from underground. The villages are the objective and social domains; the depth dimension is the stream. Now imagine further that the stream is fed by an aquifer, and that this aquifer provides the residents of the two villages with the water they need for survival. This image captures the double nature of the depth dimension. It is its own separate and equal domain—where the stream emerges--and it is also the source and seat of self—the life force that animates everyone. The divine lives inside the depth dimension, and the divine infuses all.

Where Magic Happens

Miracles are associated with the divine. And like the divine they are the stuff—the immaterial stuff!—of the depth dimension. This is so because consciousness—awareness—is the *prima materia*, the alchemical "first matter," of the depth dimension, and it is consciousness that makes miracles, and magic, happen. If we are to take the Bible literally, Jesus walked on water and rose from the dead, and what made these miracles possible was His unique (and divine) consciousness, which transformed physical matter.

But you don't need to believe in Christ or miracles to know that magic happens. Consider, for instance, the findings of the respected Princeton Engineering Anomalies Research (PEAR) program, which specializes in the scientific study of consciousness-related physical phenomena. Over the course of twenty years, PEAR has conducted thousands of experiments involving millions of trials, in which people attempt to influence a variety of physical processes by willing a specific outcome. According to PEAR, "In unattended calibrations these sophisticated machines all produce strictly random outputs, yet the experimental results display increases in information content that can only be attributed to the influence of the consciousness of the human operator... The observed effects are usually quite small, of the order of a few parts in ten thousand on average, but they are statistically repeatable and compound to highly significant deviations from chance expectations."[8]

If the PEAR findings seem improbable, it may be because we are uncomfortable with the notion that consciousness can directly affect matter. We don't want to accept that consciousness can be so powerful, or that nature, which after all is "only" physical, can respond to our intentions and emotions as if it had feelings and intelligence. Can pure depth-dimension consciousness reach out, so to speak, and transmit its desires to the physical world? Unlikely as it may seem, the PEAR research suggests this is so. The depth dimension is a magical, even miraculous, place.

The Unconscious and the Shadow

In the twentieth century, a new way to characterize the depth dimension emerged. It came to be called the "unconscious," a term that branched into two quite different meanings: repressed personal memories—the familiar Freudian sandbox filled with early-childhood bowel movements and other unappetizing stuff—and also the "collective unconscious," a term coined by the psychologist Carl Jung to describe an inventory of powerfully evocative psychological images that have come down to us over time. According to the Jungian view, the serpent and the tiger are not only real-life creatures: they also live as archetypes inside our souls, whence they migrate into our art and dreams. When we go onto the couch, whether it is a Freudian or Jungian one, it is the depth dimension we are exploring.

A related Jungian term is the "shadow," the basket of qualities we resist acknowledging about ourselves. They are our "filthy little secrets"—and secrets, as we shall see, make their home in the depth dimension. This shadow is often projected onto other groups: many people find it much easier to project negative traits onto Jews or blacks (or whoever) than to acknowledge those traits in themselves. People's refusal to acknowledge their shadow has caused many of the most horrific outbreaks of mass violence in history. And that shadow inhabits the depth dimension.

The Mythic Imagination

Among the many different categories of archetypes are the gods of the ancient pantheons, who embody qualities of personality in their undiluted form. The Greek god Ares represents the warlike instinct distilled down to its essence. Aphrodite is female sexual desirability in its unadulterated (though often adulterous) aspect.

In ancient times these qualities were honored through the worship of the gods. That fell out of fashion with the rise of Christianity. In due course it became heretical to worship any gods other than the one authorized by the Christian authorities. But while archetypes can be suppressed, they cannot be killed off. Like the gods who embody them, and like the depth dimension which contains them, they are immortal. Today, the ancient gods still resurface regularly, usually in caricature form. Pamela Anderson is a contemporary variant on Aphrodite, while the Worldwide Wrestling Federation does a rollicking business in Mars knock-offs and divine whores.

Specific archetypal images—Buddhas in a Taliban-ruled Afghanistan, for instance—can be suppressed by cultural sanction. Not the archetypes themselves, though, which continue to reside inside us.

The depth dimension is where the mythic imagination lives.

The Home of Secrets and the Wound

The unconscious is, by definition, invisible. So, as a rule, is the divine. Some lucky souls live illuminated by the glow of God, but they are the rare exception. The depth dimension is in this sense home to the unseen, to all that cannot be apprehended by the five senses. And so it is where we go to make the invisible visible.

This is, of course, what artists do: their social function is to bring hidden truths to light. From the novelist Vladimir Nabokov:

> "Yes, artist. I'm an artist. I suppose you think
> you're an artist. Many people do."
> "What on earth is an artist?"
> "An underground observatory," said Van
> promptly.[9]

"Underground," as in the depth dimension.

"Making the invisible visible" is inherently subversive work, and it is not just artists who do it. Anyone who makes a practice of dragging cultural skeletons out of the closet—the progressive railing against social injustice, the investigative journalist exposing corruption in high places—is mining the depth dimension. They are serving society, but the secrets themselves—the rips in the cultural fabric—lie hidden in the depth dimension.

Increasingly, environmental advocates find themselves cast in this role. We are in the midst of a vast ecological meltdown, yet that reality is largely disregarded by mainstream media and decision makers. Species are being exterminated at a record rate: the biologist Peter Warshall calls it a "species holocaust." Yet we cannot hear the death cries of these animals: it is occurring beyond the reach of our senses. Culturally we have buried in the depth dimension the devastation we are wreaking on the world.

Not every depth-dimension secret is cultural, though. It also harbors personal secrets, and when these personal secrets are allowed to fester they become wounds. All of us—some more, some less—live inside two stories. There is our public story, the story we feel comfortable taking out into society, and there is also our private story—feelings or beliefs we hesitate to reveal. At a men's group meeting several years ago, a question went around the room: What was our "secret truth"? Several people answered, "I'm unworthy of love." That is a very basic wound.

It is a commonplace of therapy that we heal our wounds by sharing them with others. Twelve-step programs, encounter groups, and the like all work from the same assumption: you heal your wounds by dragging them out of the depth-dimension darkness into the society light.[10]

The Home of Freedom

The depth dimension also houses our sense of freedom.

Whereas the objective domain holds our capacity for linear mental operations, and the social domain is where our impulse to subordinate ourselves to the requirements of the group reside, the depth dimension is where the free self thrives. For some this is a spiritual pursuit ("I found God and He set me free"), while for others it is a strictly secular activity (New Hampshire's motto is "Live free or die"). The spirit of liberty makes its home in the depth dimension.

In this respect, too, the depth dimension is subversive. For nothing threatens tradition and authority more than freedom.

And so, in one of the basic tensions of the triad, the depth dimension and society are continually facing off against each other in an uneasy tug-of-war that pits chaos against structure, individuality against conformity, freedom against obedience.

A Lunar, Feminine Place

Where the objective domain favors hierarchy, the depth dimension favors horizontal structures. Where the objective domain is masculine, *yang*, the depth dimension is feminine, *yin*—and a quite specific sort of feminine at that. Whereas the female aspect of society has a nurturing quality, the feminine aspect of the depth dimension is more erotic and autonomous. Feminine depth-dimension energy is lunar compared to the more solar energy of the masculine, objective domain. In times past, this energy has been associated with witches, hence the compulsive persecution of women as part of the systematic suppression of the depth dimension. Thousands upon thousands of women have been killed as witches since the Middle Ages.

In recent years, a host of books has emerged on the difference between men and women's communication styles.[11] One of the main thrusts of these works is that men are likelier to be more logical, problem-solving, and even legalistic in their orientation, while women are more interested in relationship. For instance, if a woman recounts a plight she's in, a man is likely to try to solve it, while a woman will be more inclined to listen silently. This is to say that men are biased toward the objective domain, while women tend to talk to connect, not strategize. Objective versus depth dimension: this is the ancient dialogue between men and women.

The depth dimension resists the power relations that are intrinsic to the male-dominated, hierarchical world of society. In this sense, too, it is rebellious. The Bible's intuition—"the meek shall inherit the earth"—emerges from the depth dimension. No alpha males (or females) here. Egalitarianism, not hierarchy, rules. Everyone is created equal in the eye of God—and God, as we have seen, inhabits the depth dimension.

With its bias toward egalitarianism and its generosity toward the "wound," the depth dimension tends to attract people who are uncomfortable with power. Not that the depth dimension is an ego-free zone. One can have an intense will to power and identify primarily with the values of the depth dimension. For many devotees of the depth dimension, however, the will to power is haunted by self-doubt and ambivalence. This is one reason progressives so often stumble in the ungenerous world of politics. Being conflicted about power is like overthinking during a sword fight—the Machiavellis of the world will quickly run you through.

The Experience of Authenticity

We all have our stories, our ways of giving our lives meaning and purpose. I love my wife. I am committed to helping make the world a better place. These are two of my stories, and happily they have held up pretty well.

All of us, however, have experienced stories that went wrong.

Last night Jill thought she was in love: this morning she sits across the table from last night's prince and knows differently. Inner experience is a hall of mirrors. How can we know what is genuine? How can we tell fool's gold from real? There are no empirical tests for this. Our only recourse is the depth dimension. And so we go there not only for meaning, we also go there for the experience of authenticity. The depth dimension tells us what is real, not objectively—that is the objective domain's job—but in terms of what we feel.

True, we are always at risk of waking up the next morning to find the rug pulled out from under our supposed certainty. The light is always shifting in the depth dimension. But in the search for authenticity, there is nowhere else to go.

Our Connection to Nature

Finally, we experience our connection to nature in the depth dimension.

For many in today's world, our deep dependence on the natural world is not immediately apparent. The human community seems self-sufficient and self-contained. We live in cities and buy our food in supermarkets. Television and the Internet enfold us, weaving an endless stream of information into a sheath that is more womb than web.

Seen through the lens of the triad, there are two explanations for our estrangement from nature. First, the balance inside the social domain has shifted. In our daily lives, our awareness is focused more and more on the affairs of society, and correspondingly less on the world of nature. This is an "intra-domain" imbalance, but no less critical for that.

Our cultural suppression of the depth dimension reinforces this view. We are biased toward the objective, and this teaches us to separate the observer from the observed, the self from physical nature. This distinction is illusory. We participate in nature deeply. In fact we *are* nature. And the awareness that this is so—more precisely, the *experience* of this being so—inhabits the depth dimension.

If a symbol for the objective domain is the straight line (for "getting there fast"), and symbols for society are the stage (for where we "show up") and the tribal fireplace (for the nourishing warmth of community), then an icon of the depth dimension is the web. Nature surrounds us; it contains us; it connects us. Its power and majesty wildly exceed our capacity to imagine them. No matter what the objective domain tells us, in the depth dimension we are definitely "smaller than it."

Indigenous peoples are intimately familiar with this experience because they do not live dominated by the objective domain and have direct, unobstructed access to the depth dimension. This is why they generate such strong emotions, and are both admired for not having lost touch with their true essence and looked down upon as "primitive" and "uncivilized." Children of industrial culture look at them and see what they are not, and respond with longing or contempt. What does it feel like to understand, at a bodily level, how fully we "live inside nature?" What is the experience of feeling "smaller than it?" Many people assume that First Peoples can answer these questions better than they. And to be sure, for most of us, phrases like these are abstractions. Living as we do inside the tyranny of the objective, our connectedness to nature has become a largely theoretical construct. A distant memory. A secret.

The Voice of the Depth Dimension

"What is a man? A miserable little pile of secrets."
—André Malraux

"I would rather live in a world where my life is surrounded by a mystery than live in a world so small that my mind could comprehend it." —Harry Emerson Fosdick

"You see things as they are and ask, 'why?' I dream things as they never were and ask, 'why not?'" —George Bernard Shaw

CHAPTER 4:
A SYSTEM BADLY OUT OF BALANCE

Triad Dynamics

In Chapter 3, we examined the three domains separately. Here, we consider the dynamics of the triad as a whole. The strategist, the citizen, and the seeker do not stand on their own; they are part of a system whose main features can be summed up in the following three principles:

1) *The triad is an archetypal design template for our created world.*

2) *The domains are equally valid but we play favorites.*

3) *We also long to harmonize the realms.*

The Triad Is an Archetypal Design Template for Our Created World

The triad underlies how we organize many intellectual and psychological constructs. Of the many examples I might have chosen, here are a few. We can begin with the familiar distinction between the natural sciences, the social sciences, and the arts/humanities:

- The natural sciences belong to the objective domain—their goal is to determine the objective nature of reality.
- The social sciences are about better understanding social interactions, that is, the world of the social domain (albeit through a lens heavily tinted with objectivity).
- The arts and humanities explore the world of meaning—the depth dimension.

Or take the writing arts. There are three basic types of writing—*expository*, *dramatic*, and *lyric*. Each makes its home in a different domain:

- *Expository* writing comes out of the objective domain: it presents a linear, rational argument.

- *Dramatic* writing focuses on society: it portrays what happens when people interact. The dramas it describes emerge from the clash of characters.

- *Lyrical* writing drags the elusive forms of the depth dimension into the light. It attempts to give them shape and substance.

Schools of psychological therapy also lend themselves to alignment with the triad:

- *Cognitive therapy* occupies the objective domain. According to one view, it focuses on changing "automatic thoughts (that) are frequently based on faulty logic or errors in reasoning. Cognitive therapy is directed, in part, at helping patients recognize and change these cognitive errors...In cognitive therapy, patients are usually taught how to detect cognitive errors and to use this skill in developing a more rational style of thinking."[12] A "rational style of thinking"—there's the giveaway. That's objective thinking.

- Therapies like *transactional analysis* are centered in the social domain. As articulated by Eric Berne, this approach proposes that we internalize the social roles of parent, adult, and child—the parent is punitive and controlling, the adult mature and reasonable, the child fun-loving and playful—and then act out these roles in what Berne calls "transactions" with each other. There are six basic types of transaction: parent-parent, parent-child, parent-adult, adult-child, adult-adult, and child-child. We relive our social experiences internally, Berne is saying: in psychological parlance, we "introject" them.

- And then there is *depth psychology*, which comes in a dizzying array of variations: humanistic psychology, gestalt psychology, Jungian psychology, transpersonal psychology, past-life therapy, and more. The starting-point for all these approaches is the same. It is assumed that there are depths to the self—depth as in "depth psychology," depth as in "depth dimension"— and that these depths must be plumbed for the self to be healed. The secret must be revealed, the wound made visible, else we are condemned to struggle along inside the armor of our pain.

๛๛๛๛๛

Our personalities build off the triad, too. For instance, my friend Eugene Gregan, who painted the ink-wash of the man reaching a blind hand into the depth dimension, is himself an unabashed citizen of that domain. Gregan was born with the umbilical cord wrapped around his neck; he almost died, and he believes this is why he has gone through life as an ecstatic, always reaching out for the moment of maximum connection, of maximum inspiration. Gregan is living on found money. Life is a fluke, a lucky break, so why not play it to the hilt?

Gregan is a radical libertarian and a dramatic risk-taker. He has spent much of his life not knowing where the money for the next month's rent is coming from and not worrying much about it. One of his favorite lines is, "Live in discovery!" He is that archetypal character he painted, forever reaching a blind hand into the depth dimension.

As the depth dimension is to Gregan, the social domain is to another sort of person. We're all familiar with the stereotype of the society matron, as embodied by the actress Margaret Dumont in *Animal Crackers* and other Marx Brothers films. Perle Mesta, the American socialite and diplomat who served as U.S. minister to Luxembourg from 1949 to 1953, is another well-known model of the type.

These are historical personages, but the society-centered personality is by no means a creature of the past. I was involved for a time with a woman whose mother plainly viewed it as her main function in life to keep the social wheels greased; she was an unpaid professional at the art of making conversation.

And of course we all know objective-centered folks, people

who live in their head. My father, for instance. He wasn't a nerd or egghead; he had excellent social skills and was rather athletic too. Still, intellectuals are intellectuals. He took up golf late in life, and watching him wield a golf club was almost painful. One could almost see his mind guiding his body through the prescribed motions. *I think, therefore I swing...*

❧ ❧ ❧ ❧

The triad also underlies our politics.

The objective domain is home to "liberalism" and the "left"—"L-words" that have been anathematized in recent years by the shift of the political center to the right. Old-style liberalism, which emerged out of Enlightenment values, prizes reason in its many manifestations—as technological development achieved through the application of the scientific method, and also as management, especially *rationalized* management, management that has been optimized to produce predetermined and presumably desirable results. If one only thinks things through enough, the logic goes, one can plan one's way to a predictable and positive result. In this way, liberalism bleeds into socialism and communism, both of which take as their starting point the proposition that a fully rationalized social structure can be created from the top down. For much of the last century, Soviet Russia was the land of the five-year plan, and although the plans never had much connection with reality, each new round of efforts was sustained by the irrational belief that this time around, life would finally take the hint and stay out of the way.

Even liberalism's celebrated readiness to tolerate free speech, no matter how absurd or offensive the utterances may be, flows from its faith in reason. The underlying assumption is that if people aren't hampered in their access to information and opinions, they will, as my father liked to put it, "separate the bullshit from the bull."

Where the objective domain is liberal, society is conservative. Its gods are tradition and authority. The *status quo*—the hierarchical, male-dominated status quo—is seen as good, and the institutions that represent the status quo—family, church,

52

government—are seen as good, too. Praiseworthy values and practices are those that preserve these institutions, while objectionable ones corrode them or try to tear them down.

Conservatives also believe in the power of reason, but they have less faith in people's ability to be reasonable when left entirely to their own devices. Their choices are likely to be wiser, it is felt, if they are supported by some oversight and control, ideally through the internalized injunctions of tradition and authority.

The depth dimension contains values commonly associated with "progressives," which I use in a different sense from "liberals." For some time now, the familiar left-right continuum has not accurately depicted the actual political map. There is a third center of gravity, and it embraces progressive values that are distinct from those of the old-left. Environmental protection, human rights, and women's rights are among the causes these "new progressives" have taken up, and while old-style liberals favor these causes too, something fundamentally different is at work here. As children of the sixties, the new progressives are deeply distrustful of the objective status quo and keen to explore just about anything, so long as it qualifies as alternative. Alternative medicine, alternative education, alternative nutrition, alternative spirituality. They also embrace such things as flat organizational structures, consensus decision making, and cultural relativism, all of which represent ways to break away from hierarchical, Eurocentric, dead-white-male thinking. In all these ways, their attitudes reflect hostility toward the objective domain and identification with the depth dimension.

A label has come into being in recent years to describe these new progressives. It is "cultural creatives," so named because these are the people who are said to be creating the culture that is emerging phoenix-like from the ashes of modernism. According to social researcher Paul Ray, who created this model, there are three main subcultures in the U.S.:

- *Moderns* are our yuppies. "They are the people who accept the commercialized urban-industrial world as the obvious right way to live."[13]

- *Traditionals* are, more or less, your standard-issue conservatives. They want the world to be as they imagine, say, Kansas to have been in the late nineteenth century.

- And then there are the *cultural creatives*, the folks with new-progressive values.

The triad maps onto this model perfectly. Moderns are people whose values land them in the objective domain, traditionals embrace society, while cultural creatives embrace the values of the depth dimension. Ray also identifies a divide that pits the old culture, moderns and traditionals together—the tyranny of the objective, in other words—against the avatars of the emerging culture.

Whatever nomenclature we use, this is an intense and vitally important confrontation. The emerging values of the depth dimension have elicited a hostile response from defenders of the status quo. Partly this is because anything new and important will inevitably inspire people to haul out their cudgels, and partly, it must be said, because it has been earned. In the departments of many universities, new-progressive values have hardened into an oppressive political correctness, while elsewhere it has shown up as the metaphysical excesses of the New Age. Both schools of thought, if that is what to call them, leave much to be desired. And unfortunately, they have become stalking horses for those whose enemy isn't only political correctness or the New Age, but new-progressive values generally.

Oddly, although depth-dimension values are front and center in the culture wars, they haven't established much of a presence in our political conversation, which continues to be fixated almost exclusively on the familiar, if substantially incomplete, left-right continuum. Politically, we now have a three-player contest, with two main dynamics. One pits the rationalist liberals of the objective domain against the traditionalists of society, and the other has the new progressives of the depth dimension facing off against the representatives of the objective and social domains, who are working in concert to defend the old ways. But the mainstream media largely misses the double nature of our political conversation.

Both divides are hugely important. The choice between Gore and Bush was not a choice between Tweedledum and Tweedledee, Ralph Nader's celebrated comment notwithstanding. Unlike President Bush, President Gore would have signed the Kyoto Protocol, and over the years this would probably have saved billions of dollars and millions of lives. Savings like these are not to be brushed off lightly.

Still, Nader's hyperbole is understandable. The changes our society requires run much deeper than anything Democrats or Republicans can supply. In this sense there is only one truly momentous divide, only one truly vital political conversation. The divide is between the objective domain and society on the one hand and the depth dimension on the other, and the conversation is about the suppression of the depth dimension—how to end this suppression in our psyches, our institutions, and our culture, and where to go from there.

The Realms Are Equally Valid But We Play Favorites

Each realm has its rightful place and purpose. Pursuing goals, participating in society, and making meaning are all, in this sense, created equal. Not in our psyches, though, where we play favorites with a vengeance, raising up the domains we identify with and disdaining those we don't.

There was, for instance, the time a friend of mine, a classics professor, started railing against mystical revelation. His response took me aback, though I had no illusions about how cerebral he was. I had expected that, as a classicist, he would be somewhat sympathetic toward the occult tradition, which played such a prominent role in ancient Greece. Yet here he was, mouthing the word "mystical" in a tone dripping with contempt. Eventually I came to understand his attitude: he was an ideologue of the objective domain and hostile to the depth dimension. At bottom his attitude was tribal: stay true to your school.

The depth dimension is an equal-opportunity scapegoat; partisans of society despise it too. Robert Bork, the former Supreme Court candidate and notorious arch-conservative, is such an individual, and the depth dimension plainly outrages him. In *Slouching Toward Gomorrah: Modern Liberalism and American Decline*, Bork sympathetically cites a critic who denounces rock'n'roll as "subversive of all authority, that of Western democracies, bourgeois families, schools, and churches."[14] All pelvic energy and jungle drumbeats, it is plainly a creature of the depth dimension, this rock'n'roll, and this troubles Bork greatly. Talk about your proverbial menace to society!

One hastens to add that partisans of the depth dimension play the same game, too. New Age sorts, for example, who identify with the seeker, most definitely qualify as inhabitants of that domain. Although they sing the praises of being "non-judgmental," a lot of them are mighty good at passing judgment, and what gets their goat most of all are the twin vices of "being stuck in one's head" (inhabiting the objective domain) or being "too into power and control" (society).

These realm wars dot the psychological and political landscape, and as if this weren't bad enough, they feed another unfortunate attitude as well. Having decided that the objective domain, or society, or the depth dimension, is superior to the other domains, people then decide that the ideal society is one that is inhabited by like-minded—or rather "like-realmed'"— people, and no others. This is the Henry Higgins fallacy I noted earlier.

An acquaintance once commented that she would like to run a bar/café that was designed for what she called "People Like Us." She even had an acronym for it: "PLUs." For her, this establishment would be a microcosm of the ideal society. What could be more revitalizing, what could be more fulfilling, than to be in the company of people like oneself? Hers was a utopian vision, in fact it was your basic utopian vision, the same one that has fueled innumerable social experiments in this world and fantasies about the next one.

Unfortunately this fantasy does not exactly celebrate diversity, and that makes for a bit of a problem, especially among progressives, where a commitment to diversity is de rigueur.

I became aware how true this is when I consulted in the mid-nineties with a planned community called Civano. A public-private partnership with the city of Tucson, it was designed to significantly reduce resource consumption and other environmental impacts. It was also designed for livability, with neighborhood centers, narrow streets that discourage auto traffic, and houses situated so as to encourage contact among neighbors. It was to model, in short, the sustainable community of the future.

As the project evolved, it soon became clear that many of the people who were drawn to it were of two minds about what they wanted Civano to be. On the one hand, they wanted it to be diverse and inclusive. These are, after all, progressive values, and these people were dyed-in-the-wool progressives. But Civano also represented a sanctuary of sorts. After years of feeling like outsiders in an alien culture, they would finally get to be among people who really understood them. In Civano they would get to call the shots and create their own perfect little world. It would be their shining city in the desert.

This was a perfectly understandable longing but it was also a pure expression of the Henry Higgins fallacy—*"Let's have everyone be like me."* This attitude is in a sense strategic: its appeal lies in the fact that it seems to offer people a way out of realm wars—simply steer clear of people with different domain allegiances! Out of sight, out of mind, and all that. But it is wildly escapist and ultimately ineffectual.

We Also Long to Harmonize the Realms

Realm wars are pervasive at every level, from the biliously personal to the broadly philosophical. Yet we also long to resolve these tensions and to have the realms live in harmony.

Many of our psychological strategies are directed toward this goal. Irony, for instance, can be seen as a way to resolve the ongoing tension between the objective and depth domains. Let's say I am suffering from unrequited love. Someone launches a paean to romantic bliss. "Right, love is the root of all happiness," I comment ironically. This patently false statement is a way for me to distance myself from my painful feelings. It allows for detached, objective observation—*love hurts*—without entirely relinquishing the dream of passion requited. Irony is a balancing act, a way to acknowledge the depth dimension without drowning in it.

In the end, though, irony is an ineffectual strategy. It plays to the crowd and doesn't really resolve anything. The tension between the domains may be released in a puff of wit, but it is back again moments later. Other strategies are more ambitious. For instance, romantic love seeks to integrate society and the depth dimension by creating a partnership of two (a microsociety) in which the two partners affirm the deepest level of the other's story (the depth dimension). And meditation attempts to infuse our worldly activities (society) with the "be here now" resonances of the depth dimension.

Art also tries to reconcile these tensions. A few years ago, my wife Deborah and I took a drumming class from a teacher specializing in Afro-Cuban drumming. His name was Carlos Valdez, and he was very down on music that had instruments playing in lockstep with each other. "It is a conversation between the drums," he asserted. "Each drum has its own voice. Call-and-response, call-and-response. Drumming is a language. A song is what arises out of patterns of call-and-response. Not even a solo is truly solitary. It is part of a language, part of a pattern of call-and-response."

What Valdez was saying, if I understood him correctly, was that drumming was not just an exercise in self-expression, that is, not just a communication from the depth dimension, but a social act as well: it was part of a public conversation. There was individuality in drumming ("each drum has its own voice"), but it was also participatory, part of a collective and communal language. The Afro-Cuban drumming tradition resolved the natural tension between society and the depth dimension, and for Valdez this was what made it special.

We look to resolve these tensions in our stories, too. In the movie *A Walk on the Moon*, Diane Lane plays Pearl Kantrowitz, the loyal and restless wife of Marty Kantrowitz, a likeable but uninspiring television repairman. Both have made considerable sacrifices in their lives, due largely to the arrival, when Pearl was only seventeen, of their daughter, now an adolescent in full bloom. It is 1969: freedom is in the air. Pearl has an affair with a handsome traveling salesman while the family is vacationing in the Catskill Mountains. They go off to the nearby Woodstock festival together, where the bare-breasted Pearl is spotted by her daughter, who also has sneaked off to the concert. The tension between Pearl's hankering for freedom and Marty's sense of dutifulness, between her newborn attachment to the depth dimension and his fealty to society, seems to have their marriage doomed, but it is salvaged by a luminous two-way compromise: Pearl gains a greater appreciation of her husband's heroism in having sacrificed his own future for their family— he had dreamt of being a scientist—and straitlaced Marty expresses a belated willingness to let his hair down and get a bit adventuresome. The movie ends with Marty switching the radio from a station playing frumpy music to one blasting out Jimi Hendrix's Purple Haze. He takes an awkward stab at free-form, sixties-style dancing, and after a pause Pearl joins in. Thus society and the depth dimension are reconciled. And Pearl and Marty, we are left to believe, just might live happily ever after.

And then there is the brilliant film noir *L.A. Confidential*, which tells the story of two police officers, Bud White (played by Russell Crowe) and Ed Exley (Guy Pearce). White is impulsive, moved easily to violence, all depth-dimension id. Exley is careful, calculating, ambitious. He is a committed careerist, at home inside the objective domain. Much of the dramatic tension lies in the conflict between these two men, who as the story progresses come to despise each other deeply. Theirs is a realm war: the depth dimension versus the objective domain.

When, toward the end of the movie, the tension between the two is resolved in a dramatic confrontation and they decide to work together, the mood shifts immediately. From that moment on, *L.A. Confidential* is a buddy movie, only it's not your typical buddy movie, it's a buddy movie with real depth and power because the protagonists, and the audience with them, have had to travel through a realm war to get there. With White and Exley together at last, the depth and objective domains are finally aligned, and the viewer's response is an exuberant "hallelujah!" *L.A. Confidential* is a story of redemption, of the triad made whole, of the world made right again.

This sort of longing isn't new. Two centuries ago, the visionary artist William Blake conceived a world in which there were two characters, "Los" and "Urizen." Mythologist Robin Larsen explains:

> Blake creates his own personal world in which there is "Urizen," your reason who is the god of the Old Testament and the god who measures out the universe, who says, "This is the way it's all laid out." But he gets cold and frigid and stuffy, if he's got the whole thing to worry about. And then there is "Los," this Blakeian "blakesmith"—a daemonic figure who is the poet and artist; Los is passionate, and he breaks all the bounds. Los arises out of the depths of hell, which is the only term Blake's world had for the underworld and the unconscious. But it is also a smithy, where, in the hellfires, art and passion are forged. Ultimately, Los and Urizen come together, and there is a new birth out of them: a beautiful shining child born out of their interaction. This is the hieros gamos for Blake, the marriage of heaven and hell.[15]

The story of Los and Urizen is about the integration of the powerful, analytical energy of the objective domain with the chaotic, erotic energy of the depth dimension. When the two are not equal partners, the result is servitude. In harmonious co-creation they generate the experience of paradise, or the "marriage of heaven and hell" in Blake's terminology.

<p align="center">~~~~</p>

At the archetypal level of the triad, then, our psyche is in constant conflict. Even as the domains battle for supremacy, we long for harmony, stability, mutual support and reinforcement, and even bliss. It is a tension, moreover, that is recapitulated at every level of human experience, from the interior to the interpersonal—my relationship with my father, for instance—to our institutional engagements, to our broader political and cultural environment.

At all these levels, there is a clear tendency on the part of the objective domain to assert control:

- At the interior level, this tyranny takes the form of not honoring our own authentic experience: the journey toward self-actualization is in many ways a journey out from under the thumb of the objective domain.

- At the interpersonal (and also the broader institutional and social) levels, the struggle for women's rights is really a struggle against male, that is, objective-domain, domination.

- At the institutional level, today's role model is the global corporation, an objective domain institution and power player par excellence if ever there was one.

- Culturally, the mainstream political discourse heavily favors the objective domain at the expense of the depth dimension.

How did we come to this? It is an interesting question—and a critically important one too, for this is a story that's being told here, and it is our stories that shape our strategies, and our strategies that shape our future.

Our Story So Far

Wired for Survival

We can begin our tale where things so often begin, with sex. Some time ago, I was chatting with an attractive woman when it became clear to me that I had a choice between two types of eye contact. One was oblique and a bit guarded, the other straight-on and exposed. It was the difference between society and the depth dimension, the difference between getting along and getting down. I could keep things socially appropriate or go galloping toward the Land of Eros.

The encounter left me with a revelation of sorts, and it was not about me or my libido, but the triad. One's mode of eye contact is neither casual nor coincidental; it is the visible front end of an entire neurological structure. The eyes are wired directly into the brain: if my eye-contact is oblique, that is because the pattern of neural firings that is shaping my psyche in that moment requires it. Similarly for the more naked eye-encounter: it too is backed by its own electro-energetic structure. Each of the three domains has its own characteristic pattern of neurological organization.

This train of thought led me to wonder why, from an evolutionary perspective, these three modes of neurological organization had come into being. Once I had asked the question, the answer seemed obvious: survival. We are programmed to seek survival at two levels—tribal and individual. One requires self-sacrifice—*I will die for my country!*—and the other self-assertion—*I will prevail and live on!* Our society self is committed to *collective* survival; the depth dimension is committed to *personal* survival. We experience the depth dimension as, among other things, spirituality, sexuality, and aggression (the id). It is probably not a coincidence that the longing for personal survival underlies all these impulses. Spirituality has at its heart the search for eternal life. Sexuality is about making children—biological life-after-death. Aggression is about conquering the enemy so you don't die.

From there it was a short step to concluding that where *loyalty* is one of the core values underlying society, *lust*—the lust for personal survival—is one of the drivers of the depth dimension. And the objective domain? The objective domain, I decided, is a sort of technology, one that the forces of loyalty and lust decided long ago to share in a sort of bipartisan accommodation. It is a runner, a clever servant whose sole job it is to craft strategies for survival—collective on society's behalf, individual on the depth dimension's. It is the equivalent, inside the human psyche, of the so-called spiders that scamper around the Internet running information errands. It devises ways to survive.

This character was the strategist, and in significant measure, the story of human history is the story of his rise to power. We can even date his first appearances on the mythological landscape. In Greek mythology, Prometheus stole fire from the gods. This was *logos*, reason, the strategist's special skill set. In the Bible we read: "In the beginning was the Word." Since language emerges from the objective domain—it is probably our most basic way of breaking down our life experience and making us "bigger than it"—life began, the Bible is telling us, with the emergence of that domain.

The Strategist Takes Over

From those distant beginnings we travel forward to the present day. Over time this servant, this technology, developed a characteristic neurological pattern all its own. It developed its own unique way of being in the world, its own personality. As this happened, the strategist laid claim, perfectly understandably, to being the equal of society and the depth dimension; and then, because it was so clever, it gradually took over. It is a story that has been retold again and again—as the Golem, as Frankenstein, as Hal the computer. The servant, the machine, that aspires to be master.

Modernism, which is generally thought to have emerged about four centuries ago, heaped great gobs of fuel onto the

Promethean fire. The scientific method, dualistic thinking, the separation of mind and matter (as in Descartes' famous "I think, therefore I am")—these were all variations on a theme, all ways to pursue our blossoming relationship with the objective domain. A new love affair had been launched, a love affair with objective thinking, and it was a love affair that was to alter the course of history. Suddenly reason was not simply useful, it was institutionalized. Exalted. Deified, even! The Enlightenment's light, and it was powerful indeed, was the light of objective reason.

At the time, this was a wholly positive development. Before modernism came along, the dominant ideology in Western societies was Christian dogma, whose enforcers colluded with the secular authorities to suppress free inquiry, along with all the wisdom and progress it might generate. The Enlightenment undid this, to its everlasting credit. It overthrew the rule of religion and made reason king instead. But that enthronement came at a price. Religion was confused with spirituality and as a result, in the course of throwing religion off its pedestal, modernism subjected the entire depth dimension to attack. An entire way of being in the world, an entire mode of psychic organization, was rejected. Out went the mythic imagination; out went our sense of connectedness to nature. The depth dimension was collapsed and the gold of meaning was dragged into the objective domain. *Logos* was no longer just the word of God; now it *was* God, too.

Since then, our prevailing cultural story has been that King Strategy—reason, the objective domain—will solve all our problems. Only now, from the heights of a new millennium, we can see this is not so. Reason has turned out to be a double-edged sword. It has brought us much that is wonderful, and to the brink of ecological collapse as well. Our current course is unsustainable and so is the worldview that guides it. We must release the notion, or better said, the story, that reason can conquer all.

If modernism had left the triumvirate of the objective domain, society and depth dimension intact, history would have taken a different turn. But it didn't. It hacked a leg off the tripod. Modernism wasn't magnanimous and it wasn't selective. It was barbarous. It burned the depth dimension village and enslaved its women. The masculine tyranny of the objective took over, and energies vital to emotional and ecological health went underground. And that, for the most part, is where they remain today.

This is more than unfortunate. It is disastrous. We need these depth dimension energies to save us. We need to rescue them from the objective domain where they have been locked away like a fairy-tale princess in a tower. We need to forge a new story that redeems the depth dimension. And we need to go on from there to engage the world in a way that equally honors the strategist, the citizen, and the seeker.

తతతతత

These are the truths to which my journey has brought me.

As for my father, he represented—embodied, even—the best and noblest aspects of the objective domain. His doctoral dissertation was called *The Faith of Reason*. His role model was the strategist, and his life was devoted to transporting the lessons of reason into society. In the process he bypassed the depth dimension, in fact he rejected it entirely, both at the archetypal level and in the person of his son.

Yet it is precisely this same depth dimension that we need to awaken, in ourselves and others, as a first step to revitalizing our culture and the planet.

This, then, is our conversation. It is not a private conversation, though, not just about him and me, whose lives, as Humphrey Bogart famously said, don't amount to a hill of beans in this crazy world of ours. It is about where, and what, we have come to as a species. It is about my father and me as actors in a drama that has been thousands of years in the making, about us as ambassadors representing divergent views that badly need to be aligned. When I imagine reconciling with my father, it is of course about making things right between us, but more fundamentally it is about our acting out at the microcosmic level what is required on an incomparably vaster level to make things right with the world.

Whether the characters in the story are Exley and White, or Frankel *père* and Frankel *fils*, or whoever, the underlying story is the same. Los and Urizen, the marriage of heaven and hell, the world made right again.

PART 2:
A Culture in Crisis

CHAPTER 5:
THE TYRANNY OF THE OBJECTIVE

Castles of the Intellect

Several years ago, I attended a colloquium on environmental ethics at a college not far from the Hudson River town where my wife and I live. Two Ivy League professors were the featured speakers. I was looking forward to a memorable evening. The subject of environmental ethics is important and highly charged, and I expected to come out of the session brimming over with fresh thoughts.

The colloquium did turn out to be memorable, but not in the way I expected. It was a disheartening evening, an object lesson in how the tyranny of the objective dominates conventional thinking.

The first speaker, a professor of philosophy, was heady, obscure, and self-absorbed. Not once did he make eye contact with his audience. I soon stopped trying to follow his argument and watched with a sort of distressed fascination as he followed his train of thought from station to station, losing more and more passengers along the way.

The second presentation, by a Yale professor, was troubling for a different reason. The speaker, a lawyer and political scientist, spent most of his time discussing legal strategies for increasing environmental accountability among corporations and other institutions. An important subject, to be sure, and he was a more engaging speaker—but he was talking about tactics, not ethics.

Muted applause followed their remarks. Then came the question-and-answer period. A dapperly dressed, heavy-set fellow stepped to the microphone. He was Timothy Weiskel, the director of Harvard University's Environmental Values and

Public Policy program, and he didn't pull any punches. He told the speakers he had found their comments boring and irrelevant, and charged them with a "total collapse of the imagination."

His indictment was harsh, eloquent, and accurate. The imagination is the organ of the depth dimension. Collapse the depth dimension and imagination collapses too, in which case you're left with what we were subjected to that night—two men locked in a windowless room, slaves to the objective domain.

Slaves to modernism, too. The art historian T. J. Clarke has written: "It [modernism] points to a social order that has turned from the worship of ancestors and past authorities to the pursuit of a projected future—of goods, pleasures, freedoms, forms of control over nature, or infinities of information." Clarke then adds, tellingly: "This process goes along with a great emptying and sanitizing of the imagination."[16]

That had been the giveaway for me—the two academics' "total collapse of the imagination."

I drove home that evening with the image of a chasm in my mind. As conversations at the post-colloquium reception had made abundantly clear, the attendees, students mostly, had felt frustrated and betrayed, but the two presenters had seemed oblivious to this. What for them had been high-level discourse, the audience had experienced as claustrophobic prating.

This minor mind-chasm then opened out to a larger one. These were Ivy League professors, which meant they had succeeded magnificently according to the rules of the game. Yet they were also badly out of touch, with their audience and also, more broadly, with their time. These lords of the objective domain were locked in a ramparted castle—the castle of the intellect, the castle of instrumental reasoning, the castle of society success—while throughout the land the fruit lay withering on the vine.

What would my father have thought of them?, I wondered. At the dinner table when I was growing up, Dad had groused more than once about colleagues at Columbia who he felt had lost track of what really mattered. They were too caught up in departmental politics or in conceptual frameworks that had little to do with the real world. Over the years I gained the impression that in ways he felt isolated at Columbia. He felt too much the man of action, too much the man of the world. In the acknowledgements section of *The Democratic Prospect*, he thanked his colleague and mentor Ernest Nagel for helping him "to continue to think that it is not entirely inappropriate for a contemporary philosopher to interest himself in some of the substantive problems in the world around him."[17] He might be a professor but he was not the ivory-tower sort. He had charisma and connected with his audiences. Had he been on the dais this evening, it would have been a much more engaging evening.

A man of affairs? Yes. And singular charm? That too. Yet he was also very much an advocate of the objective domain. We all have memories of our parents that still make us wince, and as I entered the last leg of the short trip home, one came to mind. I was in my early twenties and clinically depressed—a hellish condition that thankfully passed in a few months. I felt sluggish and immobilized, as if tethered by invisible ropes. This frustrated and annoyed my father. He was by nature ebullient and action-oriented, and it troubled him to see his son, whom he badly wanted to be made in his image, so gloomy and inert.

It was summer. I was living at home prior to heading off to law school, and so he received an extended exposure to my moping. One afternoon, I offered that although I knew my psyche had an "on" switch, I just couldn't seem to find it. My father threw up his hands in exasperation. "Use your will!" he exclaimed.

I couldn't, of course. That is precisely what makes depression so insidious: it immobilizes the will. My father couldn't understand this, though. The will, as he had used the term, is a tool of the objective domain. It is a very yang sort of determination, short-term and staccato. Say it is the late afternoon and I am feeling tired. Will is what gives me the resolve—the *sitz-fleisch*, my father would have called it—to stay at my desk until the job is done. Or maybe I am lifting weights. Will is what enables me to make the one last thrust that gets the dumbbells over my head. Depression is a mighty deep pit, though, and I could no more rely on my will alone to clamber out of it than I could fly to Mars. My father could not understand this.

This was part and parcel of his broader blindness to the depth dimension. That same summer, I tentatively ventured that I might possibly benefit from psychotherapy. My father, who had no patience with Freud or any of that depth-dimension lot, scowled. "What will you do after that doesn't work?" he asked brusquely.

He meant this as a criticism of psychotherapy, but I felt criticized as well. I felt challenged in my sense of who I was, in my sense of what my soul needed, in my all-too-fragile sense of authenticity. And of course no one could wield a bludgeon more effectively than my father, this icon of a culture and in many ways still my hero, this smashing success who dazzled everyone he met.

I could have taken many things from his comments. Love and concern were there, and under different circumstances I might have heard them. Instead I was left with an abiding sense of the gap that separated this man, with his empty advice and glib disdain, from his son who, as this encounter had again demonstrated, plainly inhabited an alien and illegitimate universe. And so, for a time, my depression remained.

Wherever You Go, There It Is

The two professors, and my father too, were heirs to a great tradition. Over the course of the last four centuries, the objective domain has been first discovered—a wonderfully positive development, one of the great discoveries in the history of humanity—then ennobled—appropriately, given the objective domain's capacity to do good—and finally, in a disastrous wrong turn, granted tyrannical authority. This is modernism's story, and it is producing a real-world wasteland.

Today, the values and biases of the objective domain pervade virtually every aspect of our culture. Ours is the age of science and industry, and both stem from the objective domain. "We must put nature to the rack," Francis Bacon said, in a phrase that chills the hearts of contemporary environmentalists, although in fairness it must be said that his remark was more pro-science than anti-nature. The rack he was referring to was the scientific method, and he was suggesting that observation and analysis are superior to hearsay and superstition. He wanted objective logic to replace blind faith, and this is hardly something to criticize him for, considering that all around him the Inquisition was burning people for heresy.

In business, the objective domain was the inspiration for the factories of the nineteenth century, the assembly line in the early twentieth century, and for more recent innovations such as "just-in-time" manufacturing. More broadly, it underlies industry's virtually monomaniacal emphasis on efficiency, which is all about "getting there fast," a core motivation of the objective domain.

Industry's insensitivity to the depth dimension at times defies plausibility. The industrial designer Amory Lovins recounts the time he and the writer Paul Hawken were chatting with executives at Monsanto, which was aggressively peddling genetically-modified organisms around the world. The managers proudly recounted the company's plans to sell modified bovine growth hormone, which increases milk production in cows, in the Indian market. Lovins and Hawken looked at each other. Then Hawken said, "Um, have you ever heard of 'sacred cows?'" The executives stared back blankly. Monsanto hadn't given a moment's thought to the status of cows in Hinduism.

In education, the objective domain is reflected in the assembly-line way in which children are passed from grade to grade and finally out into the world of "productivity." In higher education, it shows up in the extent to which academic disciplines are specialized. It is also instructive that it did not occur to educators to quantify students' performance until 1792, when an otherwise obscure Cambridge University tutor named William

Farish invented grades. According to Neil Postman, "[H]is idea that a quantitative value should be assigned to human thoughts was a major step toward constructing a mathematical concept of reality."[18]

A mathematical conception of reality is an objective one. The objective domain is the land of quantity, the depth dimension the land of quality. Farish substituted the former for the latter, and we have been grading students ever since.

As developments like these were elevating the objective domain, parallel efforts were underway to suppress the depth dimension. Consider, for instance, the sad story of *anima mundi*, the world soul. It is a quintessentially depth-dimension concept: it assumes that nature is after a fashion alive and informed by what today's environmentalists think of as Gaian consciousness. For millennia, it was taken for granted that *anima mundi* had a real-world existence. But then it was killed off in the seventeenth century, as modernism was coming into full flower. The cultural historian Thomas Berry writes: "[The] idea of a world-soul, an *anima mundi*, continued in the European world until the seventeenth century with the Cambridge Platonists: Henry More, Richard Cumberland, and Ralph Cudworth."[19] Stripped of *anima mundi*, nature was reduced to empirical matter—a world without soul, ripe for the rack of objective analysis.

This historical trajectory has produced a culture with a pervasive pro-objective bias, which surrounds us more than ever today. This predisposition shows up in many ways. Consider, for instance, drugs. Coffee is the drug of the objective domain: it revs up the intellect. Alcohol is the social lubricant par excellence. It's what we consume when we want to have a rollicking good time in society. And then there are marijuana and the entheogens ("god-facilitating" substances, so-called because they are said to occasion primary religious experiences) such as psilocybin, peyote, and LSD. These drugs don't merely heighten conventional reality, they alter it, quite dramatically sometimes. They are the drugs of the depth dimension.

Which of these drugs are illegal? We all know the answer to this one: marijuana and the entheogens, the drugs of the depth dimension. Regardless of its proscription, pot happens—over one-third of the U.S. public has smoked marijuana at least once, twenty million Americans smoke it every year, and two million do so daily—but that hasn't kept it from ranking high in our pantheon of cultural taboos.[20]

And then there is the extent to which our culture favors men over women. "Patriarchy" and "tyranny of the objective" are not synonymous, but they do have much in common. Male domination is *objective* domination: "patriarchy" is a subset of the tyranny of the objective.

This same bias is reflected in our communication protocols. For instance, if you want to get corporate executives and Wall Street financiers to take sustainable development more seriously, you'd better talk the masculine language of the objective domain. You've got to translate depth-dimension passion—desperation, even—into the proverbial "business case." From an article in the now-defunct *Tomorrow Magazine*:

> *A survey of the financial community in 1993 showed that environmental pleas were not heeded because they were [viewed as] too emotional. Says [Francis] Sullivan [of the World Wide Fund for Nature]: "Seven years on we've learned our language was too strident, hysterical even. It's about substantiating and quantifying, not value judgments and feelings." At a WWF seminar about investment in forests, scheduled for investors in New York later this year, the core theme will be shareholder value. "If you don't quantify," Sullivan shrugs, "that audience couldn't care less."*[21]

Quantification—that's mathematical. It's the language of the objective domain.

The same bias affects people's salaries. If your work is associated with the objective domain, you're probably overpaid. Wall Street lawyers, corporate executives, and stockbrokers all do objective work and their pay scale ranges from generous to obscene.

Move from the cognitive to the caring professions, from the objective domain to society, and salary levels plummet. If you're in a nurturing job—teacher, social worker, nurse—you're probably underpaid. (And it's probably not a coincidence that these positions are typically held by women.)

Doctors tend to be very well compensated, which says something about how they are viewed—as problem-solvers, not caregivers.

The same structural biases can be found within specific job categories. For example, although teachers are uniformly underpaid relative to many arguably less useful professions (lawyer, stockbroker, etc.), university professors tend to be better compensated than their K-12 cohorts. Why? Because their work is viewed as more purely intellectual, as more objectively oriented. Similarly, when a lawyer commits to public service, his or her salary shrinks dramatically. Government lawyers (district attorneys, Justice Department counsel, etc.) are compensated in the normal-mortal range, while Legal Aid attorneys are grossly underpaid. Economically, just about everyone who commits to the social domain gets short shrift.

As for the depth dimension, here it's a completely different game. Artists aren't salaried employees: the motif of the treasure-hunt holds sway. When we reach that blind hand into the depth dimension, it's a crap-shoot. Sometimes we come up empty, sometimes with meaning, and sometimes with real, as distinguished from symbolic, gold. One doesn't commit to the depth dimension to get rich—we are all familiar with the stereotype of the starving artist—but sometimes it happens. Artists get lucky sometimes. Live by the brush, die by the brush.

And if you want a safe, fat income, head for the objective domain.

How to Displace the Depth Dimension Without Really Trying

In its devaluing of the depth dimension, the objective

domain has a sidekick—the social domain. Extroversion, not reflection, is valued in society—and extroversion is where the action is these days. This is the age of the extrovert, in the United States especially. The spirit of gregariousness is everywhere triumphant: consider the salesman peddling the next great thing, the rock'n'roll star baring his chest to his adoring audience, the overweight member of the underclass spitting out her confession on TV. Ours is a culture that rewards exhibitionists and glad-handers, and even when our behavior is more muted, it remains the prevailing assumption that our worth is defined by our social interactions. We make or break it on the stage.

As a nation we are forever reaching out, and largely indifferent to looking within. We are like a teenage boy with too much testosterone, a shortage of self-awareness, and an incurably innocent impulse to move forward. There is something charmingly ingenuous about this, but it is also a deeply troubling quality in a global leader. It regularly produces muscular, boneheaded missteps, and since we are disinclined to learn from our mistakes, we repeat them over and over again.

Unfortunate as this is, it is hardly surprising that we act like adolescents: we are a young country, after all. And in this young country, society—extroversion—rules. Culturally we are as blind to introspection as teenagers are to the elderly.

Thus, in the U.S., advocates of the depth dimension have twin tyrannies to confront: the *yang*, Mister Fix-It mindset of the objective domain, and the national ideal of the hail-fellow-well-met. This makes for a brutal one-two punch.

This can easily seem like overkill, especially when you consider that we humans don't really need any cultural overlay to devalue the depth dimension: it's something we can do perfectly well on our own. The depth dimension can be a frightening place, not only for its horrors but also for its delights, which sometimes seem too intense to bear. And so, as part of our ongoing love-hate relationship with that domain, we develop ways to steer clear of it. One particularly popular strategy is projection, the unconscious practice of "ascribing to others one's own ideas or impulses, especially when such ideas or impulses are considered undesirable."[22] We've been "committing" projection since long before the tyranny of the objective embedded itself culturally. In fact, myths themselves are projections! From the *Oxford Dictionary of Creation Myths*:

> A myth is a narrative projection of a given cultural group's sense of its sacred past and its significant relationship with the deeper powers of the surrounding world and universe. A myth is a projection of an aspect of a culture's soul. In its complex but revealing symbolism, a myth is to a culture what a dream is to an individual.[23]

When the ancient alchemists tried to turn lead into gold, they were "committing" projection, too. Although many of them didn't realize it, the gold they were trying to create was metaphorical—the gold of self-actualization. They were externalizing the hero's journey process, transforming the depth-dimension search for self into a pseudo-science, projecting onto physical matter what was really a soul-process.[24]

Today we do something similar in our malls, where we scour the stores, searching for the great buy, the special deal, the serendipitous discovery that is our consumer-culture equivalent of the archaic buried gold. Consumerism is our contemporary version of the original alchemical confusion, our way of projecting the search for meaning onto physical stuff. It projects the material of the depth dimension onto the artifacts of society.

Naturally, the tyranny of the objective is only too happy to reinforce our impulse to suppress the depth dimension. One way it does so is through advertising. The depth dimension is irrepressible; it cannot be eliminated. Its energies can, however, be relocated, and this is what much advertising sets out to do. As physical artifacts, products inhabit society, but they are often marketed for their capacity to satisfy the depth-dimension appetite for meaning. Indeed, the very essence of consumerism lies in this: it transfers depth dimension yearnings into products.

Consider, for instance, the advertisement I saw plastered on the side of a telephone booth in New York City. "The evening began with a bottle of Cuervo and ended with vows of silence," the text read. "Vows of silence"—that's monk-talk. Alcohol takes us to God, or at least that's what the ad seemed to be saying. Cuervo was peddling tequila as a source of depth-dimension spirituality.

In a similar vein, a couple of years ago Starbucks ran a series of advertising posters in its coffee houses promoting the depth-dimensional impact of its Tazo tea ("the reincarnation of tea"). One poster showed a middle-aged Asian gentleman in casual Western garb sipping the tea, an ecstatic look on his face. "Enlightenment shall be yours," the text proclaimed. Another featured a bearded Indian saddhu. He too looked blissed-out. "Be entirely pleased," the text read.

These advertisements tell us the same thing: you too can experience the depth dimension! But only by partying with Cuervo, or drinking Tazo tea.[25]

Naturally, all this badly diminishes our depth-dimension sense of authenticity. When subjective experience is replaced by physical stuff, the gold of the heart goes wanting. One result of this is that, as a culture, we get confused about what authenticity means. Consider, for instance, the table-top advertisement I recently saw in the Cincinnati airport, at a bar named Cheers after the long-running television show of the same name. It was selling reproductions of the artifacts on the program. The placard featured a picture of Cliff, one of the show's characters, and had him saying: "These are more than your everyday souvenirs, my friend. These are authentic reproductions of the actual artifacts found in the archetypical American libation parlor."

Okay, let's take a deep breath and look at these sentences again. The products being sold are "authentic reproductions," the joke being that "reproductions" by definition can't be authentic. And not only that, they are modeled after "actual artifacts" from a bar that never existed.

What we are left with, then, are inauthentic replicas of non-existent products, which are being peddled for their authenticity, that is, for their proximity to a spiritual or emotional Source. Someone somewhere has a sense of humor.

The Experience Economy

Not only advertising trivializes and displaces the depth dimension. Sometimes entire product and service categories do too.

Maybe an entire economy, even. In a 1998 *Harvard Business Review* article, consultants Joseph Pine II and James H. Gilmore argued that commerce has passed through three stages—agriculture, industrial products, and services—and is entering a fourth, which they dubbed the "experience economy":

> How do economies change? The entire history of economic progress can be recapitulated in the four-stage evolution of the birthday cake. As a vestige of the agrarian economy, mothers made birthday cakes from scratch, mixing farm commodities (flour, sugar, butter, and eggs) that together cost mere dimes. As the goods-based industrial economy advanced, moms paid a dollar or two to Betty Crocker for premixed ingredients. Later, when the service economy took hold, busy parents ordered cakes from the bakery or grocery store, which, at $10 or $15, cost ten times as much as the packaged ingredients. Now, in the time-starved 1990s, parents neither make the birthday cake nor even throw the party. Instead, they spend $100 or more to "outsource" the entire event to Chuck E. Cheese's, the Discovery Zone, the Mining Company, or some other business that stages a memorable event for the kids—and often throws in the cake for free. Welcome to the emerging experience economy.[26]

This is both new and not-new, actually. Businesspeople have been peddling depth-dimension experiences for years. The

Halloween fun house delivers an adrenaline rush, the brain-wave stimulator an alpha-state purr, the tearjerker movie access to our sentimental emotions. But if Pine and Gilmore are correct, these historically incidental market activities are coalescing into a meta-trend.

If this is so, it is happening because human experience has become so superficial that an entire economy is organizing around the delivery of depth. The marketplace, in other words, is responding with its usual vitality to the fact that at a deep soul-level, people are hungering to get in touch with their long-lost depth dimension. They feel trapped in an unreal movie (which, no coincidence surely, is the message of movies like Woody Allen's *The Purple Rose of Cairo* and Peter Weir's more recent *The Truman Show*).

If the products and services that were being introduced had the goal of delivering genuine authenticity, that would of course be a cultural breakthrough. But that is seldom the case. What we are getting is ersatz depth instead. In their article, Pine and Gilmore provide some examples of businesses where the experience is the thing:

> At theme restaurants such as the Hard Rock Café, Planet Hollywood, or the House of Blues, the food is just a prop for what's known as "eatertainment." And stores such as Niketown, Cabella's, and Recreational Equipment Incorporated draw consumers in by offering fun activities, fascinating displays, and promotional events [sometimes labeled "shopper-tainment" or "entertailing"].
>
> But experiences are not exclusively about entertainment; companies stage an experience whenever they engage customers in a personal, memorable way ... For example, a Minneapolis computer installation and repair company calls itself the Geek Squad. Its "special agents" costume themselves in white shirts with thin black ties and pocket protectors, carry badges, drive old cars, and turn a humdrum activity into a memorable encounter.[27]

There are other examples too, most conspicuously in Las Vegas, which over the past decade has transformed itself into a sort of grand mall of pseudo-experiences. Step right up and have your Arthurian experience (Excalibur), your Arabian experience (Aladdin), your circus experience (Circus Circus), your Egyptian experience (Luxor), your pirate experience (Barbary Coast)! It's enough to give a person a grand mall seizure.

And then there is the following example from the so-called real world—specifically, Albany, New York:

> *Theme parks, theme stores, theme restaurants. Donald Metzner has a new one for the list: theme auto dealership.*
>
> *The service department of his family's Armory Automotive Family dealership now opens into a glitzy two-story atrium with shops selling car kitsch the likes of Grand Prix tire clocks and NASCAR sneakers. A giant spark plug and fan belt loom overhead and vintage gas pumps crowd the floor. Café customers eat burgers and fries on seats made of tire rims. And, of course, sale cars are on display.*
>
> *The eight-month-old Armory Center is an auto dealership as a mall. It's a place to buy lunch and a lube job, have a car wash and a manicure. It's a place to shop, listen to a jazz band or maybe just hang out.*
>
> *Sound loopy?*
>
> *Consider that car dealers around the country have been experimenting with the same sort of sizzle as Armory— although usually on a much smaller scale. Like others in the industry, Metzner believes that dealership profit margins will tighten with the rise of Internet car sales. He conceived the $6 million Armory Center as a unique way to draw and preserve customers.*
>
> *It's supposed to work like this: service and car wash customers have a place to be entertained and spend money, while others drawn to the attraction will unavoidably notice the cars for sale.*
>
> *"We're doing everything we can to bring the customer*

back as often as possible," Metzner said. "People want to be entertained."[28]

Needless to say, these enterprises are peddling a simulacrum and not the real thing. The Hollywood Café and the Geek Squad and Armory Automotive are not providing authenticity. They are selling fantasy, a trip. In the hands of mainstream marketers, the experience economy thus becomes an agent for the status quo. It responds to legitimate depth-dimension yearnings, defuses them, and converts them into cheap thrills and cash flow.

Rebels Without a Clue

Even people who think they're battling the system often fall prey to the tyranny of the objective; it is that blinding, that pervasive. The sustainability community provides an unfortunate example. As we have seen, what these people hope to achieve is something called "sustainable development," an unwieldy term that is generally agreed to involve the balancing of the "three E's" of economic growth, environmental protection and social equity. But does this definition really get at the problem? Not really. To understand why this is so, we must examine what brought us to our current understanding of sustainable development.

There have been roughly two stages in the history of modern environmentalism, a period that basically began in 1962 with the publication of Rachel Carson's landmark *Silent Spring*. Throughout the 1970s and the 1980s, the environmental challenge was viewed as a technical one responsive to technical remedies. This was pure objective thinking. Too much pollution in the air? Put filters on the smokestacks. Strategies were linear and limited. The problem was pollution; it had no social dimension.

In hindsight this can be seen as Sustainability, Stage 1.

This approach continued until the mid-1980s, when the conversation shifted to "sustainable development." As defined by the 1986 World Commission on Environment and Development, it was "development that meets the needs of the present without compromising the ability of future generations to meet their own needs." From this point on, the focus changed. With the lens now on development, it rapidly became clear that the issues weren't solely environmental. They were social, too. It came to be understood that environmental decline wasn't merely an "end-of-pipe" problem; it was caused by social problems like extreme poverty and the disempowerment of women. The "three E's" came into currency as a way of understanding sustainable development, similarly, the "three P's" of people, planet, and profits.

The talk turned to social equity, also to public dialogue. Terms like "stakeholder outreach" and "collaborative decision making" entered the lexicon. John Elkington, head of the U.K.-based think tank and consultancy SustainAbility, coined the term "triple bottom line," referring to the need for corporations to be accountable for their environmental and social as well as financial performance. The usage caught on.

Conceptually, this was all of a piece. The dialogue was migrating into society. This was Sustainability, Stage 2—the objective domain plus society. And with that the conversation pretty much came to an end. The sustainability community now knew what "sustainable development" meant.

Or did it? Actually, no. An entire dimension had been omitted from the conversation. The meaning dimension. Someday we may arrive at a Sustainability, Stage 3 that integrates the depth dimension into its vision and strategies, but we haven't gotten there yet. In what ways can people be supported to have a deep and authentic experience of meaning, and to do so in ways that not only do not interfere with, but actively support, the transition to a just and sustainable world? This is one of the critically important design challenges of our time, and it is one that urgently needs to be integrated into the collective conversation about sustainability. By and large this hasn't happened, although it is being touched on in the margins, for instance, by the "spirit in business" movement. It hasn't happened because the process got aborted. The tyranny of the objective held up a giant "stop" sign and virtually the entire sustainability community came screeching to a halt. How obedient, and how naïve!

How do we get to Sustainability, Stage 3? It is ultimately a matter of awareness: we must awaken from the dark enchantment. We have to see beyond the high walls that the tyranny of the objective has erected. The just and sustainable world of my imagination lives out beyond those walls, out beyond that over-sized "stop" sign in a land where the tyranny of the objective has no dominion. But we will never get there so long as we let the dominant reality tunnel put blinders on our vision.

The Fix Is In

One evening soon after I had first conceived the triad, I was sitting with my depth-dimension friend Eugene Gregan in his studio. We were drinking "smoky martinis," a concoction that substitutes single-malt Scotch for the traditional vermouth, and thus stimulated I was undertaking to express the concepts that were taking root inside me.

"There's the fix—the technical solution—and then there's the depth dimension—the meaning domain," I offered.

"Right, the fix," Eugene echoed, and in a martini moment I saw that he had understood the phrase quite differently from my intention.

I saw the best minds of my generation destroyed by
    madness, starving hysterical naked,
  dragging themselves through the negro streets at dawn
    looking for an angry fix,
angelheaded hipsters burning for the ancient heavenly
    connection to the starry dynamo in the machin-
    ery of night...

This was how the beat poet Allen Ginsburg had used "fix," and also how Gregan had understood the term, as the junkie's provisional salvation. I saw immediately that Gregan had hit the nail on the head: the technical fix is also the addictive fix! Culturally we are addicted to the objective domain.

This is a big problem, and the implications are even graver collectively than personally. Biotechnology, which has been touted as a revolutionary way to feed the world's rapidly expanding population, provides a case in point. A 1999 report out of Cornell University suggested that pollen from a widely-planted, genetically engineered strain of corn can make Monarch butterflies sterile.[29] If so, this puts the lie once and for all to the notion that we can muscle our way through the sustainability crisis with ever-increasing doses of the objective domain. Biotechnology is a brilliant exercise in objective problem solving, but that does not eliminate the risk that nature will react allergically. Nature thrives on a miraculously subtle interweaving of relationships. It is in this sense a depth-dimension enterprise and the objective domain is blind to this. Not that technology doesn't have a crucially important role to play, but we keep going to the same well to make things better, and that choice keeps making matters worse.

This seems to define addiction rather precisely. To the extent that we turn to the fix out of habit, not out of choice, it constitutes an addiction.

Circe, Cyclops, and the Dark Enchantment

Our addiction to the fix leaves us numbed to our surroundings. Sometimes, however, reality breaks through the veil and demands our attention. There was the time, for instance, I went shopping at Hannaford's, a giant supermarket on Ulster Avenue, my home town's version of that national institution, the Boulevard of Malls. (Local environmentalists refer to the strip as Ulcer Avenue.) The view from the Hannaford's parking lot could be featured in a photo essay of how the world went wrong. Wal-Mart. Sam's Club. Staples. As far as the eye can see, there is nothing but asphalt and big box stores.

I parked my car in Hannaford's gigantic parking lot and made my way into the gigantic store, where acres of products awaited me. As always, background music was playing. Usually I tune it out, but this time, for some reason, I noticed it. It was Joni Mitchell. She was singing, *"They paved paradise/And put up a parking lot."*

Joni was voicing a loud and legitimate objection to the world through which I and the other shoppers were wandering. No one other than myself seemed to notice, though, and on most days I wouldn't have noticed either. Although her voice was still there, her message had effectively been silenced. It had become a soundtrack for the long-playing drama called The Tyranny of the Objective.

And then there is the following incident:

> *LAS VEGAS, Nev. Inspector Dave Hunt is back on his beat, roaming this strange desert city on an urgent mission. He is searching for anyone wasting water.*
>
> *It is another hot, dry morning, and Hunt is wheeling his dusty truck into one of the many plush new residential communities rising up on the edge of town. He cruises past soaked green lawns that seem out of place in the scorched climate and sand-swept streets whose names sound like jokes: Breakwater Drive, Moonlight Bay, Gull's Landing.*
>
> *"You want to know what we're up against?" Hunt, an investigator for the Las Vegas Valley Water District, asks. "When I confronted one guy a while back about a sprinkler he was using, he got so angry he poked me in the chest and he said, 'Man, with all these new rules, you people are trying to turn this place into a desert.'"*[30]

This is denial, tuning out information that intrudes on our reality tunnel. It is an extreme example: it is the rare individual who forgets that Las Vegas is a desert. But the difference between people like that and the rest of us is one only of degree. Here in the developed world, we are all living inside pretty much the same bubble. So inundated are we by the trappings of modern, urban industrial culture that it becomes everything to us; we lose all sense of context. *Its* boundaries become *our* boundaries. We forget the worlds outside its walls—Mother Nature, the web of life, the depth dimension. Objective culture is like a vast theme park and we get lost inside it. Circus Circus, anyone?

Not that life inside objective culture doesn't have its rewards. Having indoor plumbing is a treat, and so are things like surfing the Web and settling down with some popcorn and one's sweetheart to a movie. But there are tradeoffs in everything we do, and the price we pay for our immersion in the objective domain is a dulling of that special depth-dimension sense of being vitally alive and part of a magical, mysterious web that resonates at many levels.

There is a mythical dimension to this. In *The Odyssey*, the sorceress Circe turns Ulysses' entire crew into pigs. They forget who they really are—sailors, adventurers—and spend their days snuffling and sleeping and generally acting swinish.

Circe's powers are greater than ever today, thanks to the wonders of modern technology. Her spells are the diversions and distractions that the media send our way. Every day delivers a new scandal, a new movie, a new crisis, a new something, and every one of these occurrences provides an excuse for fresh hollering. We are barraged with stuff, and with information, and most of all with breathlessness. The assault is relentless and it produces in us a kind of shell-shock that keeps us, like Ulysses' sailors, immersed in trivialities and removed from our true selves. We walk about like zombies, in a dark enchantment.

The soul does not succumb easily, though. Millions upon millions of people around the world feel lied to and cheated by the tyranny of the objective. For many, this sense of victimization is conscious: these tend to be the same people who rail at globalization, which is the economic arm of the tyranny of the objective. But the sense of living under a dark enchantment extends far beyond the anti-globalization crowd. Hollywood is in the business of mirroring our collective psyche back at us, and it regularly churns out movies on this theme. *The Invasion of the Body Snatchers*, *The Stepford Wives* and *The Matrix* are just a few of the many films that have been made about inhuman forces that require us to be soul-dead to get by.

The justly celebrated *Star Wars* trilogy has a similar theme: Darth Vader—the Dark Father—represents the negative, tyrannical aspect of the objective domain, while the Force that Luke Skywalker musters to oppose him is the power of the depth dimension. Nor should we overlook the recurrent story about alien abductions in which the abductees report being taken to spacecraft, strapped to tables, and having their sperm drawn from them by machines. If there was ever a straightforward account of being robbed of one's vital essence, this is it.

☙ ☙ ☙ ☙ ☙

While these stories reflect intuitions about what our techno-economic structures—consumer marketing, mass media, and the like—are doing to us, it would be simplistic to assume that if we could simply do away with these structures, we'd be done with the tyranny of the objective, too. The triad, remember, lives inside us—and as we've seen, we have a love-hate relationship with the depth dimension, such that there is a tug-of-war between our longing to experience its power, and our longing not to. We don't need to stupefy ourselves with television jingles to reduce ourselves to swinishness: we can do it perfectly well on our own. The story of Circe is a story about our capacity to immerse ourselves in trivialities, and it was written thousands of years before any of these modernist structures came along. Indeed, if the great mystics are to be believed, almost all of us live entranced to some degree. Being overly mired in the objective domain and not having full access to our depth-dimension selves is, it seems, our natural condition, and something we can overcome only through conscious, dedicated practice, and then only some of us, sometimes. But what is especially disconcerting about our current age is the extent to which the global diversion and distraction machine reinforces our capacity to diminish ourselves.

If you're at all inclined to be paranoid, this is probably where it's most justified. Sometimes it's hard not to see the worldwide consumer's paradise that globalization is sending our way as part of a willful plot by the powers-that-be to keep us stupefied. It's ancient Rome's bread and circuses again, only this time around it's *Who Wants To Be a Millionaire?*, *The Shopping Network*, and *Survivor*. It's Planet Hollywood and Disney World and the Super Bowl. It's today's sex scandal and tomorrow's war.

It is here where activism and spirituality converge, it seems to me. People have been sleepwalking—and commenting on it—since the time of Homer and the Buddha and before, since whenever it was that people first experienced mystical awakening. In this sense we have always been prone to falling under a dark enchantment. Modern technological culture—modern objective culture—has not created this dark enchantment, but its strategies and institutions support it. It supports us to be swinish, in fact it as good as tosses us head over tea-kettle into the pigsty. Globalization, consumerism, the hyperactive media, our sprawling entertainment culture: these are the objective domain's latest weapons in a battle for people's souls that has been going on since time immemorial. And they are powerful weapons indeed.

And so, when we resist the tyranny of the objective, it is not, strictly speaking, a secular act. Nor is it a purely spiritual one. It is both. It is integral. We do it for our own sake and we also do it for a greater cause. We do it because the tyranny of the objective—this lockstep marching from profit target to profit target, this compulsion to get from here to there with ever-greater efficiency, this irresistible urge to go faster, always faster—is undermining the health of all life on the planet, and this cannot be allowed to go on.

ॐॐॐॐ

In addition to Circe, a second mythical theme is lurking

beneath the surface here. Activists are increasingly wont to single out globalization as the root of all environmental and social evil, but globalization is really only a symptom—the tyranny of the objective is the underlying cause. The real problem with globalization is that it *exports* the tyranny of the objective. It globalizes the objective reality tunnel, and this is what makes it so dangerous. Ecosystems need diversity to flourish. A populace with only one lens for viewing things is like the one-eyed Cyclops of *The Odyssey*, the giant whose narrow vision brought his downfall at the hands of Ulysses.

This is the lesson the story of the Cyclops teaches us: an objective monoculture will inevitably have blind spots and these blind spots will bring it down. This wouldn't be a problem—*à bas les tyrants!*—but for the fact that in our current circumstances, it is bringing our natural and social capital crashing down too. We badly need the range of perspectives that domain diversity provides. William Blake said it all two centuries ago: *May God us keep/From Single vision and Newton's sleep!*

If it seems at all surprising that we need to reach back thousands of years, to the stories of Circe and the Cyclops, for a picture of who we are and where our dangers and salvation lie, we can take that as simply another indication of how deeply mired we are in the tyranny of the objective. Circe and Cyclops live in the depth dimension, and it is there, into the depth dimension, that we must go.

CHAPTER 6:
A SOCIETY DIVIDED

Warriors for the Status Quo

If we are to believe the mainstream media, the left and right define the boundaries of the known political world in the United States, if not globally. And indeed this is not entirely inaccurate, since progressives and conservatives do, in fact, view each other as mortal enemies and are deeply committed to bringing each other down. It is only a partial truth, though, and a conveniently partial one at that. As we have seen, there is a second political divide, and it is one that is largely hidden by our collective fixation with the liberal-conservative chasm. Even as left and right are huffing and puffing at each other's house, they are also collaborating furiously to keep the wolf of the depth dimension from their door. There is covert collusion here, with the social order endorsing and sustaining the values of the objective domain, and Republicans and Democrats alike staunchly defending the status quo.

Right(eous) Indignation

Conservatives regularly inveigh against the depth dimension, which they see as a hotbed of narcissistic self-absorption and disrespect for tradition and authority. In a best-selling book published in 1979, Christopher Lasch condemned what he dubbed the "culture of narcissism":

> After the political turmoil of the sixties, Americans have retreated to purely personal preoccupations. Having no hope of improving their lives in any of the ways that matter, people have convinced themselves that what matters is psychic self-improvement: getting in touch with their feelings, eating health food, taking lessons in ballet or belly-dancing, immers-

*ing themselves in the wisdom of the East, jogging, learning
how to "relate," overcoming the "fear of pleasure." Harmless
in themselves, these pursuits, elevated to a program and
wrapped in the rhetoric of authenticity and awareness, signify
a retreat from politics and a repudiation of the recent past.[31]*

Fast-forward to 1996 and *Slouching Towards Gomorrah: Modern Liberalism and American Decline,* by arch-conservative Robert Bork, who plainly abhors everything that smacks of the depth dimension. First, however, he takes pains to isolate the object of his ire, which he calls "modern liberalism," from the "classical" or "traditional" liberalism favored by people like my father:

> *The enemy within is modern liberalism, a corrosive agent
> carrying a very different mood and agenda than that of classi-
> cal or traditional liberalism.... Modernity, the child of the
> Enlightenment, failed when it became apparent that the good
> society cannot be achieved by unaided reason. The response of
> liberalism was not to turn to religion, which modernity had
> seemingly made irrelevant, but to abandon reason...[32]*

Rather than turn to the authority of religion (the purview of the social domain), "modern liberalism" descended (or rather degenerated) into the depth dimension. Bork continues to define his enemy:

> *"Modern liberalism" may not be quite the correct name
> for what I have in mind. I use the phrase merely to mean the
> latest stage of the liberalism that has been growing in the
> West for at least two and a half centuries, and probably
> longer. Nor does this suggest that I think liberalism was
> always a bad idea. So long as it was tempered by opposing
> authorities and traditions, it was a splendid idea. It is the col-
> lapse of those tempering forces that has brought us to a trium-
> phant modern liberalism with all the cultural and social
> degradation that follows in its wake. If you do not think
> "modern liberalism" an appropriate name, substitute "radical
> liberalism" or "'sentimental liberalism" or even, save us,*

"post-modern liberalism." Whatever name is used, most readers will recognize the species.[33]

Essentially, Bork is saying that liberalism (a stance of the objective domain) was perfectly acceptable so long as its chief virtue, reason, was "tempered by opposing authorities and traditions," that is, society. Liberalism could be tolerated so long as the intellectual inquiries it supported did not get too subversive and left the structures of authority mostly intact. With the loss of respect for authority, however, classical liberalism left its home in the objective domain and degenerated into "modern liberalism"—depth-dimension liberalism—whose defining characteristics, Bork goes on to tell us, are "radical egalitarianism (the equality of outcomes rather than opportunities) and radical individualism (the drastic reduction of limits to personal gratification)."[34]

Radical egalitarianism—that's a world without hierarchies, a world without the layering judgments of the objective domain. As for radical individualism, that's what you get when people turn inward—away from society, away from tradition and authority—to discover their meaning, their moorings.

The depth dimension is a special place. Something remarkable happens there; one's sense of connectedness with worlds seen and unseen becomes more powerful, more "soulful." Spiritual seekers will tell you this is good. They believe the ego is a shell and that the depth dimension cracks it open. We can all be made more, the logic goes, through the dissolution of the ego.

Bork is eyeing the same process but through a very different lens. What depth dimension advocates see as *dissolution*—a healthy antidote to the constraints of the objective domain—he sees as *dissoluteness*. For Bork, the depth dimension reeks of immorality. And that, in turn, makes the decision to plunge into the depth dimension a moral and political choice as much as a personal one. The individual who opts for the depth dimension takes sides, opting for individual delight over collective well-being, and this decision rends the fabric of society. This offends Bork, and although his lack of empathy is objectionable, his indignation is understandable. Selflessness and service are unquestionably virtues, and they both arise out of the desire to subordinate one's own selfish interests to those of other people and the greater group. They are society virtues, in other words, and Bork is quite right to want to defend them, along with the many other worthy society values—duty, loyalty, and rigorous self-discipline among them—that have served as moral beacons for people over time.

In *Slouching Toward Gomorrah*, Bork decries the depth dimension and the attempts of depth-dimension sympathizers to cast society in an unfavorable light. He praises "religion, morality, and law"—the structures of external authority—for their capacity to keep people from "rootless hedonism" (the depth dimension seen through conservative eyes).[35] He rails at criticisms of conventional society: "[Modern liberalism has] redefined what we mean by such things as child abuse, rape, and racial or sexual discrimination so that behavior until recently thought quite normal, unremarkable, even benign, is now identified as blameworthy or even criminal. Middle-class life is portrayed as oppressive and shot through with pathologies."[36] He defends the power and meaningfulness of quotidian experience: "Real human beings do not have any unfulfilled capacity for love, or at least not a large one."[37]

With this last assertion, Bork plants his flag squarely on the society side of a basic ideological fault-line. When I read his words, I was reminded of a conversation I had some years ago with Eugene Gregan, his wife Beverley, and my partner of the time. We were talking about families. I asked my companions what percentage of families they believed were dysfunctional. The Gregans were quick to answer: "Ninety-nine percent." My partner saw the matter differently: "Ten percent at most."

There it was, in stark black-and-white—the two sides of the divide. The Gregans' assumption of dysfunctionality sited them squarely in the depth dimension, where the secret, the "wound," is paramount. My partner was aligned with society. She believed that the family—society—was basically healthy. Standard-issue life was fine and didn't need much improving.

While I am not a conservative, I believe I understand why conservatives like Bork resist the depth-dimension view that society is intrinsically suspect, if not deviant. If my intuitions are correct, their view is informed by a deep affection for ordinary people—assuming, of course, that they subscribe to the right values. The conservative impulse is to honor them to the point, on occasion, of romanticizing them. Your average Jane and Joe are seen as able to lead fully realized lives without the need for interventions of the depth-dimension sort. What conservatives are venerating, in the end, is the dynamic interactions of people in an orderly society, and they resent the depth-dimension insistence on something more. It turns normalcy into abnormality, and when this happens, Joe and Jane are transformed into failures and life's everyday robustness becomes a bust. The divine order is offended. Small wonder, then, that Bork and his compeers protest!

These social-domain conservatives miss an important point, though. Essentially, they are asserting that everyday life—our everyday social structures, our everyday hearts—are perfectly satisfactory, thank you very much. The visible, the disclosed, is adequate and then some. They are deeply offended by the depth-dimension view, which holds that more, much more, awaits those of us who seek, that in our current state we are incomplete or unfulfilled. Ask your average spiritual seeker, and he or she will tell you that our capacity to love is indeed imperfect, that the heart *chakra* is partially or totally closed in almost all of us, and that through spiritual work we can increase our capacity to love. We all have it in us to be, say, Mother Theresas. Where conservatives are impelled by a desire for security and stability—to inhabit the world of the known—depth-dimension seekers are attracted to what's behind the scrim, to the invisible worlds of the unknown.

If "modern liberals" and conservatives have anything at all

in common, it is their propensity to be snobbish about the folks across the ideological fence. It is all too easy for depth-dimension sorts to look down their noses at the benighted society sorts who just don't get it about the need to do inner work, while conservatives, as we have seen, have very little tolerance for people who are inclined to explore the mysteries of consciousness more than passingly. For Bork, for Lasch (recall his observation that "Having no hope of improving their lives *in ways that matter* [italics added], people have convinced themselves that what matters is psychic self-improvement"), and for others who make their home in the social domain, these depth-dimension preoccupations are narcissistic nonsense.

The Rebellion of the Depth Dimension

This century has been, among other things, a dance between two forces, one dominant—the tyranny of the objective—and the other resistant—the depth dimension. Dada, surrealism, and even Freudianism were early-twentieth-century assertions of the merits of the depth dimension. In the 1950s, the beatniks laid claim to the banner of rebellion, which soon metamorphosed into the counterculture revolution of the Woodstock generation. The sixties' fire burned too brightly and flamed out. Or did it? I suspect it went underground instead, where it continued to forge the souls of many baby boomers. A great many it glazed lightly with depth-dimension consciousness, enough so they could hold their own at gatherings of cultural creatives. A handful became *bodhisattvas*.

Strange Bedfellows

Today, the rebellion of the depth dimension continues unabated. It comes in forms both metaphysical and political, and it produces some unlikely bedfellows. For instance, one doesn't usually mention libertarians and progressives in the same breath, except maybe for formulations like "libertarians and progressives can't abide each other," but they have common roots in the depth dimension.

More than anything, libertarians are preoccupied with free-dom, which they view as being under continual assault by the long arm of the state. The Libertarian Party describes its philosophy this way:

> The Libertarian way is a logically consistent approach to politics based on the moral principle of self-ownership. Each individual has the right to control his or her own body, action, speech, and property. Government's only role is to help individuals defend themselves from force and fraud.... The Libertarian Party is for all who don't want to push other people around and don't want to be pushed around themselves. Live and let live is the Libertarian way.[38]

"Self-ownership"—that's personal freedom, the right to do what one wishes with one's life. It is libertarians' most cherished value, and, as we saw in Chapter 3, its source is the depth dimension.

A great many progressives, although not all of them, also identify with depth-dimension values. Invite your average progressive to help themselves at the values smorgasbord, and they are likely to return to your table with depth-dimension dishes like the following:

- An abiding interest in things alternative—alternative medicine, alternative education, alternative spirituality;
- Sympathy for the downtrodden and the desire to give voice to the voiceless—the poor, women, the environment; and
- A commitment to consensus decision-making and nonhierarchical organizational structures.

Their shared roots in the depth dimension notwithstanding, libertarians and progressives disagree fundamentally on many issues. Libertarians want the state to get out of the way; progressives want the state to step in and save the day. Even their enemies of choice differ: for libertarians it is the society-centered state, while progressives, for the most part, fasten on big, objective-domain corporations. Libertarians and progressives do, however, have this in common: an attachment to one or more depth-dimension values.

But perhaps we should take stock of how much to make of all this. There are quite a few depth-dimension values, after all. If two people go shopping at the same store, and Jill emerges with one dress and Jane with another, this does not prove that their tastes are similar, or, for that matter, that they have anything whatsoever in common. In the unique context of the triad, however, the fact that libertarian Jills and progressive Janes both shop at the same depth-dimension store is noteworthy. What they have in common is rebellion—opposition to the status quo. The depth dimension is why people fight back, and where they fight back from, even while embracing different values and causes.

The Politics of Meaning

The rebellion of the depth dimension also shows up in the "politics of meaning," a term coined by Michael Lerner, a rabbi and the editor of *Tikkun Magazine*. Meaning, of course, is what we seek in the depth dimension, and so a politics of meaning is a politics of the depth dimension.

"A progressive politics of meaning," Lerner writes, "posits a new bottom line. An institution or social practice is to be considered efficient or productive to the extent that it fosters ethically, spiritually, ecologically, and psychologically sensitive and caring human beings who can maintain long-term, loving personal and social relationships."[39] Also:

> [P]ublic disaffection with liberalism does not mean that people want a more centrist politics or some elusive mush that the press refers to as the "moderate center." The failures of liberalism do not call for a move to the Right, nor for a move to the Left (that is, a militant revival of the old one-dimensional assumptions of an economistic and rights-oriented lib-

eralism), but rather for a move to transcend the old ways of thinking and begin to acknowledge the meaning-needs that liberalism cannot fully grasp within the limits of its existing categories. Because liberals do not understand this, they find themselves trapped in a fruitless debate between those who imagine they will be more popular by moving to the Right and those who advocate a return to a pure version of the old-time liberal or Left politics. Both views are mistaken.

Lerner is advocating a political journey south, to the land of the depth dimension.

Lerner's "politics of meaning" enjoyed a certain vogue for a time because it attracted the attention of Hillary Clinton. However, it never really made it into the political mainstream. It was a doctrine created by and for people who consciously identify with the values of the depth dimension.

Realm Wars Back at You

It is entirely understandable when people resent the injustices of the tyranny of the objective. Unfortunately, people sometimes react, or rather overreact, by giving the depth dimension privileged treatment instead. This is tyranny in reverse, and not useful.

This describes quite precisely the phenomenon known as political correctness, as it has established itself most especially in our universities. This set of attitudes came into the world as an entirely legitimate reaction to a set of social attitudes and structures that privileged white, heterosexual males to the detriment of women, people of color, and homosexuals. A great many people reacted to these pathological hierarchies by embracing flat organizational structures and rejecting hierarchy entirely. Theirs was, in this regard, a deeply depth-dimension view, and it was one in which everyone commanded equal respect, and not just the most obvious targets of bigotry, but anyone anywhere who might be low on someone's pecking order.

Our language changed in consequence. "Queers" became "gay." "Negroes" became "blacks" or "African-Americans." "Retarded" people became "developmentally challenged." And as the mood grew increasingly hypersensitive, we used the old terminology at our peril. The "politically correct" movement was like, and you should excuse the political incorrectness, a good girl gone bad. It started with its heart in the right place, and then took a wrong turn and stumbled down the road to perdition. In rejecting not just pathological hierarchies, but all hierarchy, the PC brigades denied an aspect of themselves—the objective domain—and they also, along the way, committed the perhaps even more grievous error of misplacing their sense of humor. It is ever thus when the love of justice hardens into fundamentalism, which is what happened here. The politically correct movement became imperious, demanding, and tyrannical in defense of the depth dimension.

One sometimes finds the same overreaction in progressive political circles. Again, the initial intuition is on target—it is the subsequent privileging of the depth dimension at the expense of other domains that is problematic. One cultural critic whose otherwise powerful work falls into this trap, in my opinion, is the ecopsychologist Theodore Roszak. In *The Voice of the Earth*, Roszak argues passionately, and often persuasively, for a renaissance of depth-dimension values. In that work, Roszak writes that the "core of the mind is the ecological unconscious," and goes on to argue that "repression of the ecological unconscious is the deepest root of collusive madness in industrial society."[40]

This view has much in common with my own: there are close affinities between the ecological unconscious and the depth dimension, although they are not identical—we can think of the ecological unconscious as a single room in the sprawling house of the depth dimension. Substitute "depth dimension" for "ecological unconscious"—include the entire superset, in other words ("repression of the *depth dimension* is the deepest root of collusive madness in industrial society")—and we are making the same point precisely.

At this juncture, however, our views diverge. Overall, the voice one hears in *The Voice of the Earth* is of a person who identifies exuberantly, indeed excessively, with the self-indulgent, sensual side of the depth dimension. He speaks favorably of narcissism and praises people who "goof off, make love, perhaps in public places, and think well of themselves for doing it."[41] This is the sort of thing that raises the hackles of conservatives, and it even strikes me, who strives to be open-minded about this sort of thing, as celebrating some of the less evolved and ultimately less interesting aspects of the depth dimension. It turns emotional immaturity into a species of enlightenment and, at a minimum, is a prescription for polarization.

Elsewhere, Roszak envisages revitalizing the ecological unconscious through atavistic rituals—dancing in moonlit forests and the like. The problem with this heartwarming back-to-the-garden fantasy is that it is, in the end, delusional; try as we might, we can never return to our indigenous roots by dancing in the moonlight. We are children of modernity, and while this can be pretended away for brief spells of time, it cannot be done away with entirely. We can only move forward by adding on and integrating; we cannot discard essential aspects of our experience, and it does no good to try. There is no going back again, even if our soul wishes otherwise.[42]

More broadly, Roszak and other progressive thinkers often seem to miss that the raising-up of the depth dimension must in the end be an intermediate step. The desire to rehabilitate the depth dimension is perfectly understandable, but having honored it, we must then get beyond it. We must break the spell of the tyranny of the objective by identifying with the depth dimension—and then, having done so, we must *disidentify* with it and embrace an integral perspective that values all three domains. It's either that, or realm wars.

ॐॐॐॐ

Another battleground in the realm wars is the peaceable kingdom of New Age thinking which, in its inimitably soft and "sharing" way, tilts toward fundamentalism in its embrace of depth-dimension values.

We can begin with the perhaps obvious fact that New Age thinking is a depth-dimension ideology. One indicator of this is how seriously New Agers take their spirituality: "We are spiritual beings having a physical experience," as one friend put it. More proof comes from the New Age emphasis on how free we are, if only we realized it. We can do anything we want to, if we only claim our power, New Age thinking goes. We can "create our own reality."

This is a mixed blessing, actually. If you have cancer, you created it, probably because of some unresolved psychological issue. On the positive side, however, you can do something about it—it's all in your control! Heal your cancer-causing inner wound and your tumor will vanish, too.

It is inspiring, intoxicating even, to think we have it in us to eliminate all our misfortunes—but the high comes complete with hangover. If we don't get better, it's our fault. The New Age view of personal responsibility delivers empowerment and guilt in equal measure, depending on how the dice fall. And in fact, it is not entirely within our power whether we are healed or not. Sometimes circumstances—genetics, environment, dumb luck—create our "reality." My tumor may reflect unresolved anger toward my parents, but it also may be my DNA destiny. Sometimes cancer is not a metaphor.

I think of the "you-create-your-own-reality" credo as "New Age creationism." Fundamentalists may claim God created the world, but they are wrong— you and I did!

For several years, I belonged to a men's group where New Age creationism ruled. The members were forever "creating" this and "creating" that. Their illnesses, their business woes, and more. This was a depth-dimension culture that celebrated and indeed exaggerated the power and magic of the self. At these gatherings, I was regularly exposed to how unbalanced the New Age commitment to the depth dimension can get. For example, at one of our biweekly meetings, a guy reported that he'd stumbled while climbing a set of stairs, then wondered out loud why he'd "created" that. Hey, maybe he'd just stumbled? And then there was the time another member, Joe, declared that the victims of the Lockerbie plane crash had known, unconsciously of course, that the flight was doomed and had chosen to be on it anyway. They were working through karma or some such thing, they had "created their own reality."

This one really roused my ire. Was I then to assume, I asked Joe, that the children who'd been gassed at Auschwitz had chosen their fate too? The way I saw it, we inhabited a moral universe, and Joe's New Age creationism messed with it unacceptably. It transformed guilt into a sort of zero-sum game: as the responsibility of the victims grew, the guilt of the perpetrators shrank. Now that the Lockerbie crash victims had "created their own reality," the onus was off the terrorists who had planted the bomb. Ditto for the keepers of the ovens, since the children of Auschwitz had chosen to be gassed. This was wrong. It was worse than wrong. It was outrageous.

I fulminated for a time about this, and was given plenty of space to do so by my tolerant New Age companions. We do "create our own reality," I said, but not always or entirely. Chance collided with choice at Lockerbie, at Auschwitz too.

For me, this exchange has come to exemplify how the "you-create-your-own-reality" school of thought overcompensates so badly. It is completely understandable for people to resent and resist the tyranny of the objective and to side with the depth dimension. But that does not justify making the depth dimension all-powerful. The three domains were created equal. The depth dimension, objective domain, and social domain are partners. They dance together, sometimes well and sometimes clumsily, and their dancing shapes the world.

The cosmos functions elegantly. Perfectly, even. It doesn't play favorites. We do, though, and we do so interminably and pathologically. We make the depth dimension nothing, or everything, and these choices split society in two.

Divided Loyalties

Although the New Agers overshoot the mark, they are quite right to resist the tyranny of the objective, which is at the root of so much malaise. The tyranny of the objective tells a story about who we are, and this story shapes our educational, entertainment, and economic systems; it molds our consciousness from early childhood on. While many of its values, when taken singly, are unobjectionable, once woven together into a single overarching narrative, they become a control mythology that does a gross disservice to people and the planet. This control mythology is pervasive and pernicious. It becomes the sea we swim in—and a polluted one, at that.

Yet something in the human spirit resists. Something in the human spirit understands that there is more to life than this and struggles to lay claim to its birthright, the uniquely depth-dimension experiences of authenticity and personal fulfillment. And so we find, even among those who have not consciously aligned themselves with the depth dimension, a widespread yearning for depth-dimension experiences, as well as for a political culture that fairly reflects depth-dimension values.

The Politics of Authenticity

One way this shows up is in the national fatigue with Democrats and Republicans alike, and the widespread hankering for a straightshooting, fiercely independent politician. The 1990s saw the rise of what might be called a "politics of authenticity." And authenticity, as we have seen, inhabits the depth dimension.

When Ross Perot ran for president in 1992, it was as a "people's candidate" who spoke the plain truth. It was a populist campaign, but it was a populism that had been updated to address a uniquely contemporary frustration. Historically, populism has catered to popular resentment of the ruling classes. Perot shifted the emphasis. While his campaign was by no means devoid of the old rhetoric, his main target wasn't the time-honored one of power and privilege so much as, to put it bluntly, institutionalized bullshit.

Perot understood how emotionally bankrupt the tyranny of the objective is for many people, and tried to parlay this resentment into a presidency. His calling card was authenticity—no fancy, expensive advertisements for him when simple, straight talk would do.

Next in line for the authenticity mantle was Jesse Ventura, former governor of Minnesota. There is more than a little irony in having an ex-pro wrestler serve as the repository for our fantasies about authenticity, but we have gotten to a point where people don't mind inauthenticity, so long as it is, so to speak, authentically inauthentic. When Jesse Ventura did his wrestler's shtick, he was exaggeratedly phony, and when he donned his citizen's persona, he came across as a genuine straight shooter. At least people could tell what was what that way, instead of getting caught up in the elusive no-man's land of politics-as-usual. It's ill-disguised phoniness that people are fed up with, and they see plenty of that in Democrats and Republicans alike.

If it seemed weird to see Jesse the Body run for political office, things have gotten a whole lot weirder since. In September 2002, the FX television network announced a new reality program, *The American Candidate*, to air in 2004. One hundred contestants will compete for viewers' votes, with the winner to run for U.S. president if he or she chooses.

It's hard to say if this is a horrible idea, a wonderful idea, or both. If nothing else, the fact that it seems to be reality TV's next big thing is a commentary on the extent to which the general public has come to view the current political system as bogus. "*American Candidate* could become a kind of de facto third party, but without a crazy, short billionaire Texan," opined a CNN commentator.[43] Yes indeed—and we can be pretty sure that if it does, the candidate's chief selling point will be his or her perceived authenticity.

Hollywood Goes Deep

The popular yearning for the depth dimension shows up in mainstream movies, too. For instance, in the blockbuster science-fiction movie *The Matrix*, Keanu Reeves plays Neo, a reluctant hero who learns that what he has always assumed was the everyday world is the product of a vast computer simulation ("the matrix"). The energy to drive the matrix is drawn from people who are used, essentially, as batteries. It is Neo's destiny to be the messiah who saves humanity from this efficient but unappetizing alternative to petroleum. It takes him some time to learn that he is "the One," but once he does, he starts performing miracles, for instance, by stopping bullets in midflight.

The story line is straight out of the triad. Computers are artifacts of the objective domain, and they have taken over society so completely that people have been reduced to energy sources for The Machine. The objective domain rules, society is a vampire, the human spirit perishes.

Until the new messiah comes along. Neo is the voice of the repressed depth dimension. It is his destiny to end the tyranny of the objective and show the way for people to discover their authentic selves. (No surprise here: this is what messiahs always do, guide people to their authentic selves.)

In a telephone call to the Matrix at the movie's end, Neo communicates this role straightforwardly:

> *I know you're out there. I can feel you now. I know that you're afraid. You're afraid of us. You're afraid of change. I don't know the future. I didn't come here to tell you how this is going to end. I came here to tell you how it's going to begin. I'm going to hang up this phone and then I'm going to show these people what you don't want them to see. I'm going to show them a world without you, a world without rules and controls, without borders or boundaries, a world where anything is possible. Where we go from there is a choice I leave to you.*

"*A world without rules and controls, without borders or boundaries, a world where anything is possible.*" That is the depth dimension, and Neo is the miracle-working messiah, flinging a challenge at the objective domain from its subversive heart.

The smash hit *American Beauty* has an equally strong depth-dimension bias. The story recounts the last year in the life of Lester Burnham (Kevin Spacey), who awakens from a long period of self-proclaimed "sedation" to reclaim his erotic and emotional vitality. For years, he has been confused and dissatisfied, sleepwalking through an unfulfilled and altogether too predictable life. He is awakened from his hibernation by Ricky Pitts, a fearless, precociously wise teenager who has recently moved next door and also just happens to be a marijuana dealer. At a gathering of real estate executives, where Ricky is working a catering gig, they retire to an alley where they share a joint. Meanwhile Lester's wife Carolyn, a frigid and desperately unhappy real-estate saleswoman, has been getting tipsy with the handsome Buddy Kane. In their choice of highs, Lester and Carolyn's divergent directions have been flagged: Carolyn stays with the intoxicant of society, while Lester's pot-smoking takes him into the depth dimension, a domain that, once re-engaged, soon has him feeling healthy and whole again.

Through a series of misunderstandings, Ricky's father, the homophobic and authoritarian Colonel Pitts, becomes persuaded that Lester is a homosexual who is paying his son for sexual favors. This appalls him and also awakens his own homoerotic desires. He makes a pass at Lester and is rejected. This is too much for the Colonel, who cannot abide the new view of himself in the mirror. Lester becomes all that is evil, all that is awful, all that must be rejected—in short, his own forsaken depth dimension. He takes a gun and kills Lester.

In so doing, he is barely one step ahead of Carolyn, who is also feeling alone and abandoned. She goes home, intending to kill Lester, but the Colonel has beaten her to it.

Carolyn and the Colonel are spiritual partners. Both are dutiful servants of society; both are panicky repressers of the depth dimension. Both project their shadow onto Lester. His newfound freedom summons them both to kill.

American Beauty was the great hit of 1999. Critics raved, calling it "dazzling," "mesmerizing," and "a work of genius." It won five Oscars. And it was not just a *success d'estime*: the film grossed well over $200 million, succeeding both as art film and popular entertainment. *American Beauty* was an ode to the depth dimension, and people around the world loved it.

❧❧❧❧

And so we find that society is split into three camps. We have the warriors for the status quo, opposed by the underdog warriors for the depth dimension. And then there are the many people who aren't at war with anyone, except with themselves. I think of these people as the "American Beauties," people whose political ire hasn't been especially aroused and who know only that they feel unhappy and confused. Their souls are divided between allegiance to our control mythology and to the depth-dimension knowledge that the dark enchantment it imposes is steering their souls, and the world, wrong.

The American Beauties warrant taking close note of. Not only are there a great many of them, but they are also mirrors of our culture. See them, and you see our society. America's soul is divided, too.

CHAPTER 7:
THE FITFUL SLEEP OF THE DEPTH DIMENSION

Signs of Emergence

Today's airports have a deracinated sameness, as befits these way stations of globalization. The Albany International Airport is a smallish and mostly predictable version of these ubiquitous McAirports. Travelers there will find the same basic layout and efficiently antiseptic mood as in other airports throughout the world.

In one modest respect, however, the Albany airport is different. It houses, in a rather central location, an interfaith prayer room. Not a chapel, mind you, an "interfaith prayer room." All travelers, regardless of faith, are welcome. A simple twenty-foot-by-twenty-foot space, it contains benches and a prayer rug, a water sculpture, and no religious icons whatsoever. It is not memorably beautiful or even stylish, but its purpose is clear—to serve, amidst all that hurly-burly, as a space for contemplation.

The first time I happened on this room, I was pleasantly surprised. It seemed so symbolically apt: here, in this stronghold of the tyranny of the objective, a small depth-dimension flower was blooming. Its presence, just down the corridor from McDonald's, spoke to me of a broader trend—the slow, often imperceptible, but seemingly implacable assertion of depth dimension values in the face of imperial might.

A Focus on Quality

One sign of the shift toward depth-dimension values is that traditional modes of measurement are coming under challenge. The tree of the objective domain is being shaken.

Start with the gross domestic product (GDP), which is a

wildly perverse measure of progress. When someone gets cancer, it registers as a positive on the GDP because it generates revenues for the health care industry. Oil spills drive up the GDP because they must be cleaned up. Auto accidents are great news for the GDP, too—the bigger the better, actually.

Raw dollar turnover is the only thing GDP measures. It is of no consequence whether the activities that generate those revenues point to a society that is flourishing, or one that is failing. Health, happiness, and well-being are all irrelevant. If terrorists brought down a hundred World Trade Centers and they were subsequently rebuilt to the tune of billions upon billions of dollars, that would be a cause for celebration, if we were guided only by the GDP.

The GDP is a deeply flawed metric. Something more fundamental than mere dollar turnover needs to be measured—whether our society is becoming a better or worse place. Fortunately, alternative indexes are emerging to fill this gaping void. One such measure is the Genuine Progress Indicator, or GPI. Developed by Redefining Progress, a San Francisco-based think tank, the GPI "starts with the same accounting framework as the GDP, but then makes some crucial distinctions: It adds in the economic contributions of household and volunteer work, but subtracts factors such as crime, pollution, and family breakdown."[44] For the period 1990-1997, according to Redefining Progress, as the GDP was climbing by 18.5%, the GPI actually dropped 11.6%.

What measures like the GPI do, in essence, is set quantity in the context of *quality*. Since (objective) quantity is an objective concept and (subjective) quality a depth-dimension one, what they are trying to do is integrate the objective and depth domains.

Traditional quantitative measurement is under siege in the domain of cultural preservation, too. In late 1998, the Getty Conservation Institute convened a group of scholars and practitioners for "a conference investigating economic issues relating to the conservation of heritage objects, collections, buildings, and sites."⁴⁵ Participant Randall Mason writes:

> This meeting, part of a larger inquiry into the economics
> of conservation, was designed to fill a specific absence in the
> existing body of work on economics and conservation: the need
> to investigate the concepts that have traditionally separated
> economic and cultural conservation discourses and to investi-
> gate concepts for joining them. This approach contrasts with
> the thrust of much contemporary research on the economics of
> conservation, which asks how to measure heritage in terms of
> price, without considering why.... At the heart of the meeting
> was the fundamental quandary that methods of economic val-
> uation increasingly dominate society's handling of the values
> of heritage, while the same methods are unable to account for
> some of the most salient values and virtues of heritage—
> namely, historical meaning, symbolic and spiritual values,
> political functions, aesthetic qualities, and the capacity of her-
> itage to help communities negotiate and form their identity. In
> short, heritage cannot be valued simply in terms of price.⁴⁶

Here too, the question being asked is: how do we move
beyond the quantitative, slap-a-number-on-it bias of the objective domain and integrate into our valuations those many
depth-dimension characteristics that defy quantitative measurement?

Much the same question is being asked in education. The
approach known as "lifelong learning" sidesteps the entire issue
of numeric grades by making learning a goal in and of itself,
while the emerging "alternative assessment" school offers a
portfolio of strategies for subjectively measuring the actual
learning that takes place, rather than relying on the much more
objective measures of traditional testing.

The issue here is not only philosophical. Measurement
strategies that confine themselves to the objective domain are
often inaccurate. A GDP that disregards quality of life is miss-
ing the point. So is a Scholastic Aptitude Test (SAT) that, as
now appears to be the case, cannot accurately predict academic

performance.[47]

A Culture of Disclosure

As we have seen, the depth dimension houses the wound—the secret—whence it is hauled out (or not) into the bright lights of society—the stage. What to withhold and what to disclose is a choice each of us makes innumerable times during our lives. As individuals we develop policies about this, and so, more broadly, do cultures. In Western industrial society, the trend is toward confession. The pervasiveness of electronic information technology, which makes it more and more difficult to suppress information, probably has something to do with this. The ideal of the open, democratic society does too. And so does the depth dimension's will to self-assertion.

Confessional daytime television programs—Jerry Springer, Sally Jesse Raphael *et al.*—take disclosure to its logical extreme. But the trend toward disclosure can be found in behavior that is neither so dubious nor dramatic. Consider, for instance, the ubiquitous twelve-step programs. No longer are they for alcoholics only: you can now twelve-step your way to happiness if you are a food addict, a sex addict, a workaholic, or even a plain old drug addict. And "sharing"—voluntary disclosure—is what makes all those programs tick.

Disclosure is also the driving force behind Eve Ensler's celebrated *The Vagina Monologues* and the V-Day women's awareness movement it has spawned. Here's what the feminist Gloria Steinem has to say about the play and the women's movement that preceded it:

> These last three decades of feminism were…marked by a deep anger as the truth of violence against the female body was revealed, whether it took the form of rape, childhood sexual abuse, anti-lesbian violence, physical abuse of women, sexual harassment, terrorism against reproductive freedom, or the international crime of female genital mutilation. Women's sanity was saved by bringing these hidden experiences into the

open, naming them, and turning our rage into positive action to reduce and heal violence. Part of the tidal wave of creativity that has resulted from this energy of truth telling is this play and book [The Vagina Monologues].

When I first went to see Eve Ensler perform the intimate narratives in these pages—gathered from more than two hundred interviews and then turned into poetry for the theater—I thought: I already know this: it's the journey of truth telling we've been on for the past three decades.[48]

This is disclosure as a force for personal liberation and social transformation. And of course it is not only women who are stepping forward with their suppressed truths. Other culturally oppressed groups are doing so, too.

Disclosure is increasingly the rule in enterprise as well. A landmark step in that direction was the 1987 SARA (Superfund Amendments and Reauthorization Act) Title III, which required companies to publish annual emission levels of hundreds of chemicals. No longer could companies simply pollute and remain silent: a measure of public accountability had been institutionalized. Since then, disclosure requirements under SARA Title III have been expanded—a further lowering of the walls. The recent Global Reporting Initiative, which led to the establishment of an international standard for voluntary corporate sustainability reporting, continues this trend. Plainly it is progress when corporations divulge more rather than less information, and it is just as plainly a process that begins in the depth dimension. "Sharing," that cliché of the New Age, is winning.

Storytelling and the Cultural Creatives

These are not the only signs of depth-dimension emergence. Consider, for instance, the recent upsurge of interest in story-telling. Whether they are drawn from real life or the well of the imagination, stories provide guidance about how to understand our life experience. They are tutorials in meaning.

And so our culture's heightened sensitivity to storytelling reflects, at least to some extent, a heightened sensitivity to the role of meaning—that is, the depth dimension—in shaping our "surround."

The signs of this new awareness are everywhere. "Story Hysteria," the progressive magazine *Utne Reader* trumpeted on the cover of its September/October 1997 issue, and followed the headline with this teaser: "Telling all is a national obsession. Here's how to break through to the stories that really matter." In Canada, a 1999 Massey Lecture was titled *The Triumph of Narrative: Storytelling in an Age of Mass Culture*.[49] It featured Robert Fulford, telling "the story of how stories live and breathe at the heart of our culture."

The theme of the story is everywhere. It was the cultural historian Thomas Berry who touched on it most famously relative to sustainability:

> It's all a question of story. We are in trouble just now because we do not have a good story. We are in between stories. The old story, the account of how the world came to be and how we fit into it, is no longer effective. Yet we have not learned the new story.[50]

Since Berry sounded the alarm, various writers and thinkers have moved in to fill the gap. In the novel *Ishmael*, Daniel Quinn recruited a gorilla to recount a sustainability oriented history of the world. In *The Post-Capitalist World*, David Korten tried to flesh out the story of what a society without global corporations might look like. Edward Freeman, a professor of business at the University of Virginia, is developing a new story for capitalism, which he calls "stakeholder capitalism" or "values-based capitalism":

> The idea is that what makes capitalism work is that stakeholders can cooperate to create something that no one of them can alone. The entrepreneur puts together a deal that simultaneously satisfies customers, employees, suppliers, fin-

*anciers and communities. Nothing terribly new here, except
that we need to see this new story as a fundamental replace-
ment of Cowboy Capitalism, or the "Business Sucks" story,
or whatever you want to call the view that capitalism is a
bunch of greedy little bastards trying to do each other in.*[51]

Storytelling is also gaining more prominence as a phenomenon in its own right. "Not a weekend goes by without a storytelling festival somewhere in the U.S.," reports Steve
Kardaless, the interim executive director of the Tennessee-
based National Storytelling Network. His organization
recently coordinated an international "Tellebration" that featured simultaneous storytelling festivals at 303 sites in thirteen
countries and forty-two U.S. states.[52]

This is the era of mass storytelling. Everywhere you turn
you will find another story coming at you, in movies, in books,
in television shows, and advertisements. The overall effect of
this endless blitzkrieg of stories is numbing, a combination of
both quantity—the volume is overwhelming—and quality—
most of the stories that come our way reduce experience to a
debasing two-dimensionality. This relentlessness probably goes
a long way toward explaining how sensitized people have
become to the place of storytelling in our psyches and culture.
This sensitization is also a predictable development in a post-
modern world where, it is widely agreed, there is no underlying
truth and "reality" is what you make of it.

But I suspect something else is happening as well. The buzz
about stories reflects a growing understanding that stories make
meaning, and meaning is how we construct our world, and how
we construct our world affects not only our personal happiness,
but our collective destiny, too. In this sense the New Agers
have it right: we *do* create our own reality. And so the new
emphasis on storytelling and "the story" reflects a desire,
among other things, to resuscitate depth-dimension meaning.

ॐॐॐॐॐ

If we are to believe the social researcher Paul Ray, further proof of the rise of the depth dimension comes from the cultural creatives, who, as we have seen, are advocates of the depth dimension. As laid out in the book *The Cultural Creatives: How 50 Million People Are Changing the World*, which Ray coauthored with his wife Sherry Anderson, cultural creatives comprise about one-quarter of the adult U.S. populace, and more significantly still, they are the only one of the three main subcultures that is growing—the modernists (objective values) and traditionals (society) are in decline. Ray infers from this that the cultural creatives are winning the war of the worldviews.

Ray's story has been enthusiastically embraced in the progressive community, and understandably so. It's easy for people with depth-dimension values to feel they're losing the war. Ecologically and socially, the future looks bleak, and those in power seem unwilling or unable to take notice. Under these circumstances, it is easy to despair. And then along comes Ray bearing his message of hope. His views are couched as social science but their gist is inspirational. Essentially, he is saying that the progressive movement is alive and well, and more evolved too. In its early days, progressive politics were secular, patriarchal, and class-obsessed. Now they embrace spirituality, feminism, and environmental protection. The subtext of his message is, "We are wiser, we are powerful, we shall prevail!" In a community where hope can be hard to come by, the vision of one out of four Americans being an ally, a fellow soldier in a great cause, is heartening.

But is it true? More broadly, do the depth-dimension emergents that we have identified presage a fundamental shift in our culture, as Ray believes, or is all the ado about relatively little? With these questions, we turn to the next stage of our inquiry.

A Reality Check

Put all these developments together, and we have what looks suspiciously like a trend. Some unnamed cultural force or energy—an unconscious intuition about what the times require, perhaps—seems intent on dragging depth-dimension values across the border, so to speak, into mainstream culture.

Is this assessment correct? Are the big changes Paul Ray and others envision truly in the works? This is the optimist's view, and it may be correct. But then again, it may not be. There are reasons to be skeptical.

To begin with, it must be remembered that there is nothing especially new in the tension between the depth dimension and the established order. The depth dimension has been rising, and falling, and then rising again, for millennia. The tension between self and society, between secular and spiritual authority, has been with us through much of human history. Our current cultural dynamics, the assimilation of depth-dimension values included, are part of an ancient pattern and may not foreshadow anything particularly dramatic.

A second consideration is that the incorporation of depth-dimension values into mainstream culture is by no means across the board. Quality, secrets, and story-telling are not the only items on the depth-dimension menu. Our sense of connectedness to nature, for instance, continues to be consigned to the cultural periphery.

It is also the case that depth-dimension values are sometimes adopted for reasons that are more about business opportunity than culture change. Consider, for instance, the recent trend among women's clothes designers to affix the "vintage" label to new clothes—complete, sometimes, with factory-installed gashes—and the related phenomenon of products being manufactured as collectibles—Beanie Babies, for instance. There is something deeply manipulative in this. People prize vintage clothing and genuine collectibles because they come to us from the past. They speak eloquently of time and place, and this gives them a depth and vibrancy of meaning that are absent in modern-day mass-produced products. Their value lies in their depth-dimension qualities, in other words. When "vintage" clothes and "genuine collectibles" are churned off an assembly line, we have the present doing cheap knock-offs of the past; we have the objective-domain pursuit of profits raiding the depth dimension and exploitatively churning out cheap replicas of soul.

Nor are the cultural currents traveling in just one direction. Powerful contrary winds are gusting too, directly in the face of the depth dimension. Communication technologies, and the Internet especially, are arguably the most potent agents of transformation in the world, and while they sometimes serve the depth dimension, they do much of their work in thrall to the objective domain.

The Double-Edged Sword of the Internet

The Internet is a complex phenomenon, a sort of double agent. At one level, it is a force straight out of the depth dimension. It flattens hierarchy. It supports freedom, democracy, and underground activities generally. During the Chinese democratic uprising in 1989, fax machines, a relatively feeble electronic precursor of the Internet, were one of the main sources of communication among the activists. Today the Internet amplifies that power many times over. In one memorable incident, in 2000 a group of "hacktivists" rerouted visitors to Nike's website to a grassroots-activist site protesting the Asia Pacific World Economic Forum meetings. The Internet provides cover for innumerable such hit-and-run operations. Ecological economist Hazel Henderson calls it the "jungle drums phenomenon": "You can hear the sounds everywhere but you can't locate them. And you can't cut off the heads of the leaders."[53]

Even the language of the Internet rings of the depth dimension. "The Web"—that's the web of connectedness, the primal pattern of the depth dimension.

But even as it is flattening and democratizing and generally stirring up trouble, the Internet is also doing yeoman work for the objective domain. It is first and foremost a technology, and technology emerges from the objective domain. Computer design is binary and linear. The Internet is fired by billions of tiny electronic gates, opening and shutting, signaling yes or no. It is machine logic taking over the world.

The Internet does the objective domain's work in another way, too. It pulls us more deeply into technotime. All that information ratchets our nervous systems into overdrive, inducing an agitation that eventually becomes routine. We become, as the magazine of the same name has it, "wired." Today we live in technological time, and technotime is more than an abstract concept. It is something we feel, something that inhabits our bodies.

Technotime is stimulating, it is debilitating, and it is something else as well—continuously accelerating. It is, in this regard, the opposite of the depth dimension, where the deeper you go, the more time slows down—so much so, in fact, that if you travel deep enough, you eventually experience something that feels like eternity. Technotime takes us in the opposite direction, away from our experience of God, away from the interior space where deep reflection becomes possible.

Bobos in Purgatory

The way Paul Ray sees it, the cultural creatives are the cavalry riding to our rescue. That's a bracing view if you want to believe in a positive future, and it's doubly bracing if you happen to see yourself as one of the troops in blue. That's not the only way to see these people, though. In *Bobos in Paradise*, cultural critic David Brooks paints a much less heroic picture of this group and its agenda.

"Bobos" stands for "bourgeois bohemians." We all know who these characters are, even if the term is unfamiliar. They're the male doctors sporting earrings, the bankers lounging in their pinstripe suits in espresso bars, the artists anxiously scanning their stock portfolios. With one foot in society and the other in the depth dimension, bobos are a study in contradictions. They are socially and professionally ambitious in the usual ladder-climbing way, but they view these qualities as something to be underplayed, to both themselves and the world. Their real selves, such as they are, are softer, gentler, more into caring and sharing. Bobos believe in artistic self-expression, in caring for the planet, in women's rights, in spiritual growth, in...hey, wait a minute, these are the cultural creatives!

Which is precisely my point. Are the fifty million progressives Ray identifies really cultural creatives, or are they...*the horror*...bobos? These are two different breeds of change agent, to be sure. Whereas Ray's cultural creatives are the vanguard of a brighter future—the avatars of a culture in transformation—Brooks's bobos are much more lightweight. They're not concerned with social change so much as with being fashionable in the curious, contradictory style of our era. Where Ray sees a Wagner opera, Brooks sees a Molière comedy—bobos as participants in the timeless and ultimately comical game of social striving. And while Brooks acknowledges that bobos have made the world a better place—he writes, for instance, "Shops are more interesting [and] the food in the grocery stores and restaurants is immeasurably better and more diverse"—on balance this is pretty mild stuff.[54] Certainly it lacks the gristle to transform, never mind save, the world.

Why Progressives Aren't Making Progress

Given the multitude of forces and counterforces that are in play, it is probably safe to assume that the tyranny of the objective cannot be overthrown without the active participation of a great many people around the world. This, of course, is what the progressive movement has been trying to do for years, and while from one perspective it has accomplished a great deal—there wasn't even an environmental movement forty years ago, and think how far the civil and women's rights movements have come—it is also true that all things considered, it has been glaringly ineffectual. David Orr, a professor of environmental studies at Oberlin College, is pretty much on target when he characterizes the progressive movement as being in "failure mode."[55]

There is something perplexing about this. Here we have a sizable group of people whose eyes are for the most part unclouded by the dark enchantment and who would just love to see the tyranny of the objective toppled. They have clarity and commitment going for them, and it would seem much else besides—the various indicators of depth-dimension emergence, for one thing, plus a not inconsiderable reservoir of emotional support to draw on. Even if you discount the cultural creatives as a force for dynamic change, there are still all those bobos out there, and although they can't be counted on to take to the streets for progressive issues, they're still quite sympathetic to depth-dimension values. And there are also the vast legions of people who, while not visibly bobo-esque, yearn to integrate the depth dimension into their lives. These are the "American Beauties," the men and women who, no matter how much they immerse themselves in mainstream culture, cannot silence the voice inside them whispering that the American dream, as packaged by the tyranny of the objective, is partial at best and at worst a baldfaced lie. One might expect these people at the very least to have an open mind about what progressives have to say.

Yet despite these positives, the progressive community has made precious little headway in the battle to win the hearts and minds of Americans. If there is one single explanation for this state of affairs, it is this: progressives' ensnarement inside realm wars and their resulting inability to get out of their own way.

One especially vexing internecine dispute involves the role of the objective domain. Progressives, you will recall, are advocates for the depth dimension: it is their role to unearth the secrets buried there, whether that be the injustices wrought by the powerful on the powerless, or the environmental devastation that is leaching the vitality from nature. If we take this analysis down to another level, however, we find that some progressives are quite comfortable with hard-headed, left-brained, objective-domain strategizing, while others are put off by it. The resulting clash, between what we might call the "strategist" and "seeker" factions of the progressive camp, keeps progressives at loggerheads with each other despite their shared values at another level. And this antagonism keeps the broader movement stuck in neutral.

For progressive strategists, it is not the objective domain itself that is the enemy, but its unintended consequences—excessive pollution and the like. Strategists have no problem using objective domain-inspired technologies to further their objectives. What matters is winning, and the objective domain can help enormously in this regard.

Progressive seekers view the matter differently. For them, the mindset, not its consequences, is the problem. The objective domain is itself, so to speak, a pollutant, and so it is best to shun it in the search for remedies. This is the more fundamentalist position, and it brings with it instinctive and ardent opposition to such things as hierarchical organizational structures and top-down strategies, both constructs of the objective domain.

The progressive movement is rent by this division. Over the past several decades, many national environmental groups have embraced the objective domain. Environmental Defense, the Natural Resources Defense Council, and the National Wildlife Federation are among the groups that have become significant lobbying presences inside the Beltway. Corporate spin doctors have even coined the term "multinational NGOs," suggesting that some environmental groups are as powerful (and, by implication, as dubious) as the multinational corporations they condemn.

For radical and grassroots environmentalists, the readiness of representatives of national environmental groups to sit down at the table with industrialists and other beneficiaries of the "system" makes them complicit—collaborators, even, in the Second World War sense of the term. In negotiations, in the courtroom, the trained specialists of the national environmental groups use instrumental reasoning—the logic of the objective domain—to persuade, drive bargains, and achieve legal victories. There is a compelling logic to their doing this—fight fire with fire—but progressive seekers will have none of it. The way they see it, you could put the suits of the Environmental Defense in a line-up alongside the suits of McDonald's and ExxonMobil and not be able to tell the difference.

Nowhere are the battle lines more clearly drawn than around the issue of emissions trading. This policy, which enjoys the blessing of national environmental groups like Environmental Defense, grants corporations the right to pollute, or emit certain pollutants (including carbon dioxide), up to a certain limit. Pollute (or emit) less than the maximum, and you can sell the difference to companies that are over the threshold. Thus, less pollution translates into hard dollars and this, the theory goes, incentivizes companies to improve their environmental performance. Advocates of emissions trading argue that market forces and economics—the ancient laws of the marketplace, in short—are the best (and perhaps the only) way to drive real change. Opponents like ecological economist Hazel Henderson object strongly on ethical grounds. "No one," she says, "has the right to buy and sell the right to invade my body with pollutants."[56]

The tension between progressive strategists and seekers can get quite personal. In the fall of 2002, I attended Bioneers, an annual gathering of progressives that includes a sizable anticorporate contingent. One session featured a debate between Paul Gilding, a friend and occasional colleague, and John Stauber, a freelance journalist who is best known for his anticorporate polemic, *Toxic Sludge Is Good for You: Lies, Damned Lies, and the Public Relations Industry*. The topic was whether people like Gilding, who once ran Greenpeace International and now consults with global corporations, are pragmatists serving sustainability (Gilding's view) or sellouts consorting with the devil (Stauber's). Both were committed progressives, but one was a pragmatist—a strategist—and the other was a hardcore seeker.

After the debate, I rose to ask a question. It seemed to me, I said, that Stauber and Gilding embodied two quite different mindsets. Stauber's was "either/or"—you could be *either* corporate *or* a progressive, but the term "corporate progressive" was an oxymoron. Gilding, by contrast, was arguing for "yes/ and"—there were synergies to be found in integrating the two cultures. I went on to say that I favored Gilding's position—and would Stauber care to comment?

Stauber never answered my question. Instead he denounced me, at least that is how I heard him. He suggested to the audience that I had been planted there by Gilding to make life uncomfortable for him (not true), and he also implied that I was a corporate stooge who was there to sow dissension among progressives. As evidence, he offered the facts that I have written for green business magazines and collaborated with people like Gilding.

It was, shall we say, a learning experience. And what I learned, among other things, was that it is not only conservative fundamentalists who are driven to demonize. Progressive fundamentalists do it, too. And while their putative enemy is the global corporation, I suspect that sometimes it is something deeper—the objective domain itself—that inspires their hostility.

One frequently finds ambivalence about the objective domain creating rifts at local meetings of progressives, too. Many readers will find the following scene familiar: a number of progressives have gathered somewhere, in a living room or restaurant, to decide on a course of action. Rather than launch directly into the strategizing process, they go around the table introducing themselves. By the time everyone has finished, much of the time available for strategizing has been squandered, and the meeting breaks up with a hasty, ill-considered decision being made.

It is, of course, gracious to invite people to introduce themselves, and it is often useful too, but not infrequently the ritual has another function as well. It can also be an invitation—a demand, really, couched as an invitation—to participate in a public, almost feudal declaration of loyalty to the depth dimension. It is a way to remind the attendees that at this gathering it is the whole person, not just the strategist, that counts, and that everyone around the table is unique and entitled to an equal say. There are no favorites here, the ritual announces: what is prized here is relationship, and respect for the intrinsic sacredness of everyone present, and power relationships that have not the slightest hint of "above" or "below" in them. Around this table one will find no "better" and no "worse," and most of all no hierarchies.

These are all, of course, core values of the depth dimension. The web of connectedness is being ritually woven here.

Is this useful? Sometimes yes, sometimes no. Conversations about strategic directions can get barbed; they can be better negotiated if a safe space has been created first. In my experience, though, the going-around-the-table ritual often has a different agenda, and it is one that betrays a deep ambivalence about the objective domain. It is a public reminder by believers in the depth dimension that the objective domain is to be approached cautiously: it is not entirely unlike picking up a cross before you enter a room where you think there might be a vampire.

Unfortunately, this dubiousness colors and often drags down the strategic discussion that follows. This is not a happy outcome for the local group, and it does not serve the broader progressive movement any better, for ambivalence about the objective domain breeds ineffectuality.

Things get even worse when progressives' dubiousness about the objective domain hardens into fundamentalism. Depth-dimension values are seen as indisputably good; objective values are seen as reprehensible. This is why John Stauber attacked me, I believe. And when this fundamentalism sets the tone at a local grassroots gathering, you can pretty much count on the atmosphere to be humorless and oppressive. If a person doesn't display just the right values in just the right way, the hammer of disapprobation is sure to come crashing down. And what makes this especially ironic is that the fundamentalism in question embraces a depth-dimension culture that supposedly cherishes self-expression and authenticity.

Being looked down upon for refusing to knuckle under to cultural expectations would be galling under any circumstances, and it is all the more so when it takes place at the hands of a culture that prides itself on having evolved beyond the hammer. Wielding a hammer requires you to stand in judgment, after all, and depth-dimension culture is supposed to be nonjudgmental. But just try telling that to someone who has failed a depth-dimension loyalty test and been found by the group to be wanting.

Realm wars are also a pervasive problem in the progressive community's relations with the broader world outside the trenches, which are characterized by a deeply ingrained us-versus-them bias. "They"—the defenders of the tyranny of the objective—are seen as powerful, pitiless, and unapproachable. It is assumed that it makes no sense to approach them, and so progressives turn to each other for solace instead. On the one hand, this is comforting, but it also produces an "ain't it awful" mindset that is both disheartening and disempowering. What comes next is inevitable: endless broadsides written for the true believers and hurled over the ramparts in the hope that someone, somewhere out there will happen to read it, and agree. It's a realm-war mindset, and worse still, it's a realm-war mindset with a defeatist, defensive attitude.

It is not that the progressive cause is without merit. The depth dimension *does* need to be raised up, and progressives are also correct in believing that we are in a battle whose stakes are almost inconceivably high—the right to a reasonable quality of life for future generations. Unfortunately, progressives are trapped in an ineffectual and ultimately anachronistic mode of engagement. The simple fact is that engaging in realm wars in the old-fashioned way is almost surely a doomed strategy. The corporate consolidation of media that has taken place in recent years has significantly reduced people's access to viewpoints that shine a light on the lies and distortions of the tyranny of the objective, and it has also done an effective job of caricaturing and marginalizing anyone whose views do manage to squeeze past the roadblocks. Add to this the fact that most people are so harried and distracted in their daily lives that they don't really have the time to focus for more than a few moments on anything, and we are left with the odds stacked heavily against the prospect of progressives prevailing in a battle of reality tunnels.

Does this mean things are hopeless? Has the time come for progressives to pack up their politics and head home? Absolutely not. But it is time to try something new.

๛๛๛๛

In this section, I've told a story about a culture in crisis. We've seen that the tyranny of the objective is well-entrenched and pervasive, and that it has cast a spell, a mythological "dark enchantment," over virtually our entire culture, such that many of our most pressing social and environmental issues are trivialized or disregarded. We've also seen that not even the long arm and iron fist of the tyranny of the objective have been able to eliminate many people's longing for the values and experiences of the depth dimension. At the same time, many—in fact, most—of us remain entrenched in our preferred domains and reality tunnels, and regularly engage in realm wars that are tearing society apart. Depth-dimension progressives do this; conservatives and liberals do it, too.

In the long run, this can only be counterproductive. At the overarching system level, the impulse to lock ideological horns creates stalemates and "stuckness," and these are things we can ill afford just now, as each passing day brings us closer to the ecological precipice. We need to find ways to work together. We need to route around these standoffs; realm wars keep us mired in them instead.

Something more is required. That something is the integral way.

PART 3:
The Integral Way

CHAPTER 8:
INTEGRAL ESSENTIALS

A Brief History of Integral Thinking

The integral way is a variant on a school of thought that is generally deemed to have been launched in 1949, with the publication of the cultural philosopher Jean Gebser's seminal *The Ever-Present Origin*. In that book, Gebser proposed that consciousness evolves up a spiral, that this journey progresses through an identifiable sequence of stages, and that this process recurs at different levels of complexity, from the life cycle of the single individual to the birth and death of entire civilizations.

These shifts in consciousness, according to Gebser, are profound. Today we speak of shifts in "values," and while values do shift when consciousness shifts, Gebser had in mind something much deeper than that. The journey up the ladder of consciousness entails seismic shifts in the structures of the self, such that life itself is experienced fundamentally differently.

These are the touchstones of integral thinking—a journey toward ever-higher levels of consciousness recapitulated in contexts from the personal to the cultural, with each level "transcending and including" each previous level. It posits a species that is evolving psychologically as well as physically, and doing so on a step-change basis.

For Gebser, "integral culture" was the level we are headed toward, both individually and as a culture. As he saw it, the integral structure of consciousness integrates all prior levels of consciousness, and it was also what is variously called "world-centric" or "aperspectival," a couple of two-dollar words that mean, essentially, that one no longer identifies only with one's own tribe (or nation, or empire), but with all humanity or, even more inclusively, all nature.

In Gebser's view, the integral worldview was destined to replace what he called the "mental" structure of consciousness, the immediately prior and currently dominant reality tunnel that Georg Feuerstein describes as "the domain of...the thinking mind, of reasoning in its different forms. It is a cognitive style, or paradigm, that operates on the principle of duality, or either/ or. It implies a conscious subject that experiences itself as standing apart from the objects, or contents, of awareness."[57]

If this sounds a lot like the objective domain, you're right. The triad has much in common with Gebser's framework and other integral models.

Since Gebser, the integral perspective has been elaborated by pioneering thinkers such as Clare Graves, William Irwin Thompson, and, most recently, Ken Wilber. While these and other visionaries have cogently mapped the integral landscape, it is important to remember that integral thinking is a fullblown cultural emergent and not just the purview of a few high-pow-ered philosophers. As Antony Arcari and Allan Combs point out, "The emerging integral age is not being defined by any one person or group in any one discipline, religion, political group or country. The waves of integral emergence have been felt over the last fifty years in all fields of endeavor: Science, Art, Humanities, Education, Ecology, Spirituality, Culture, Law, Psychology, Philosophy, Business, Medicine, and Politics."[58]

This is not to suggest that the integral perspective is any-where near becoming the dominant structure of consciousness. It is steadily gaining adherents and momentum, though. For those who believe that what Gebser called the mental structure of consciousness, and I call the tyranny of the objective, is the main cause of our global crisis, this is an encouraging develop-ment.

The challenge, given our circumstances, is to accelerate the pace at which the integral perspective is incorporated into our indi-vidual and collective decision-making processes. At this point, the only really useful way for integral advocates to do this is by transitioning from abstract theorizing to strategic implementation. And this is starting to happen. 1998 saw the formation of an organization called the Integral Institute (www.integralinstitute.org), supported by a million-dollar grant from the visionary entrepreneur Joseph P. Firmage and with Ken Wilber installed as president. The Institute has four goals, according to its website:

1   **Integrate** the largest amount of research from the largest number of disciplines—including the natural sciences (physics, chemistry, biology, neurology, ecology), art, ethics, religion, psychology, politics, business, sociology, and spirituality;

2   Develop **practical products and services** from this research—which can be used by individuals in their own development, or by groups, businesses, national and international organizations;

3   **Apply this integrated knowledge** and **method of problem solving** to critical and urgent issues—especially the serious political, health, educational, business, and environmental problems facing humanity; and

4   Create the world's first **integral learning community.**[59]

Ambitious and grounded goals, these. Meanwhile, as this central coordinating committee for the integral movement searches for its sea legs, initiatives are springing up in the United States and around the world that, while not always characterized as integral, bear all the hallmarks of that approach. We will examine some examples in the next chapter; first, though, it may be useful to define our terms more precisely. What I have called the integral way has a set of identifying features, just as an animal or plant species does. These features can be found no matter whose integral framework we are using—and sometimes in endeavors that haven't yet been classified as integral. And so, by way of preparing the ground for the more factual discussion to follow, let's take a closer look at precisely what it is that makes something integral.

The DNA of the Integral Way

Stripped to its essentials, the integral way is a three-part, positive feedback loop. It begins with a practice—*inclusivity*. We override our initial impulse to reject views we are inclined to find distasteful. We do our best to understand them and identify those aspects that have value and serve a purpose.

Engaged as an ongoing practice, this leads to *fundamentally new patterns of organization*, for reasons I will explain. At the personal level, we experience ourselves as somehow fundamentally different. This "new self" is the personality I have called the sage. At the institutional level, this transformation can emerge in any number of ways—as a fundamentally new vision, or a new governance structure, or a fresh set of policies or strategies.

Interface Inc. was an unremarkable floor covering company until the early nineteen nineties, when Ray Anderson, the corporation's founder, read Paul Hawken's *The Ecology of Commerce*, which lays out in devastating detail what we are doing to the planet. Anderson describes the experience as having been like "a spear in the chest" for him. He started preaching the sustainability gospel—I heard him give one speech in which he proclaimed that today's captains of industry would one day be seen as planetary pirates—and set out to turn Interface into a model of corporate sustainability. Today, the company's vision statement reads, in part: "To be the first company that, by its deeds, shows the entire industrial world what sustainability is in all its dimensions." Whether Interface achieves that lofty goal remains to be seen, but one thing is incontrovertible: Anderson's "spear in the chest" created a fundamentally new pattern of organization inside both his psyche and his company.

These fundamentally new patterns of organization, in turn, produce a variety of *benefits*, including: 1) higher-level insights into self and society; 2) an improved capacity for constructive dialogue; 3) breakthrough solutions; and 4) a powerful and more expansive new identity (personal or institutional).

A garden metaphor may be useful here. Inclusivity is like a

soil enhancer we use to enrich a garden. The resulting abundance and fundamentally new appearance of the garden constitute the fundamentally new pattern of organization (although if our analogy were completely on target, the fertilizer would support the emergence of an entirely new species of flower!). The benefits consist of the extra nutrition this abundance supplies to the garden and the broader world.

The integral way is thus an ecosystem, a virtuous cycle of positive feedback loops. It begins with inclusivity, which leads to a fundamentally new pattern of organization, which produces various benefits, which reaffirm the commitment to inclusivity. And then the process runs its loop again.

The Practice: Inclusivity

The integral way begins with a basic proposition: *instead of "either/or," "yes/and."* Rather than trying to prevail, seek common ground. Assume that you can "win" only if the other side "wins," too.

The goal is to lift the dialogue out of the foxholes. Describing Ken Wilber's approach, Jack Crittenden writes:

> The general idea is straightforward. It is not which theorist is right and which is wrong. His [Wilber's] idea is that everyone is basically right, and he wants to figure out how that can be so. "I don't believe," Wilber says, "that any human mind is capable of 100 percent error. So instead of asking which approach is right and which is wrong, we assume each approach is true but partial, and then try to figure out how to fit these partial truths together, how to integrate them—not how to pick one and get rid of the others."[60]

This is not the same as "win-win," although there are resemblances. The term, which came into common parlance a decade or so ago, is used to describe an outcome that is pleasing or at least acceptable to all parties to a negotiation. It rapidly gained adherents because it powerfully countered the notion that negotiations necessarily produce winners and losers. "Win-win" suggests you can come up with superior outcomes if you do not take a zero-sum approach and instead enter the negotiation in a spirit of mutual collaboration. That's a pleasing and important point, but also a bit shopworn by now.

The integral way expands on "win-win" in two important respects. First, as normally used, "win-win" is an objective-domain concept: it is about helping parties to a negotiation achieve their objectives. Inclusivity is fundamentally different in that it resides in the depth dimension. It describes a way of holding abstract concepts in one's inner space—your and my seemingly irreconcilable goals, your assumptions about what John and Jill and Jane hold dear, and so on. It is a way to respect the values and experiences of others, instead of responding with a knee-jerk, negative reaction. Let's say Joe is a compulsive gambler. If I am engaging him in a spirit of inclusivity, I try to get beyond the dismissive impulse I might normally be inclined to have and to understand why he finds gambling so irresistible. Inclusivity is, in other words, a *process*, and more specifically, it is a process we engage in over time. In fact it isn't just a process, it is also a *practice*, and like all practices it can change our self-sense if we attend to it diligently enough.

The word "practice" often comes coupled with another word: "spiritual," as in "spiritual practice." To say that inclusivity has a spiritual dimension may be overstating the matter a bit, but only a little. In any event, we can make our point without using that term. "Win-win" is flat. Inclusivity has *depth*.

The second difference between "win-win" and inclusivity lies in the frame surrounding the respective concepts. "Win-win" is about, well, *winning*. It's about coming out ahead in the secular world. Inclusivity is about *learning*. It is about expanding and becoming richer at the soul level. Different domains, different goals.

So that is where we begin—with *inclusivity*. One makes room in one's heart and mind for every viewpoint, including those we find distasteful.

Some people find this easier to do than others. It goes against the grain not to play favorites: it is in our nature, and probably our evolutionary programming, to do so. The integral way asks us to overcome this impulse, and to do so on an ongoing basis. This is what makes it a practice, something we must cultivate consciously.

Let me give an example from personal experience. In this book, I espouse an archetypal view of things. I position the triad as archetypal, and I also encourage people to view themselves as participants in a drama of cosmic dimensions. In addition, I espouse a self-sense in which we honor our life experiences for the passions they evoke, while also experiencing them as part of a grand historical pageant consisting of billions of such dramas, each one of which is, in the end, relatively insignificant.

This perspective elicited a range of responses when I shared early drafts of the manuscript with friends. Some saw it as psychologically and spiritually evolved, while others were less flattering. One reader viewed it as a defense mechanism designed to keep me at a safe remove from my feelings, while another found my affection for the archetypal and mythical altogether too New Age.

Instead, I did my best to practice inclusivity. I tried to treat all the views I'd heard as possible and none of them as certain. It was a sort of quantum perspective I adopted—these were all potential truths, but the emphasis was on the potential. All were to be treated inclusively, but none was unassailably true. If I had followed my instincts, I would have agreed with the favorable interpretations and dismissed the negative ones. I am a rat like the rest of us, after all, and I like to press the lever that makes me feel good.

In keeping an open mind about the feedback, my hope was that these different views would eventually coalesce into a fresh and useful perspective on the book. This, in the end, is what the practice of inclusivity is all about: it challenges us to hold the inputs we receive in a way that can potentially help us understand the subject under scrutiny differently, and perhaps more deeply.

The commitment to inclusivity is a central aspect of the sage's path, and it is one in which truth is seen not as any single view or interpretation, but as a way of holding multiple views—as a way, in the end, of engaging our life experience. It is not that the sage doesn't have clear opinions, but they are held lightly, with a deep awareness of the complex and impermanent nature of all things, including our opinions. For the sage, truth is transient and ultimately inseparable from our life process. It is a transitive verb, not a noun we've fixed in place.

When we practice inclusivity, we are actually practicing open-mindedness, and open-mindedness is not only an attitude, it is also a self-sense, a soul-feeling, and a pleasing one at that. It makes one feel light, expansive, inspired (in the etymological sense of "filled with breath"). It is what one might call a virtuous delight.

Practicing inclusivity offers a second benefit, too. By training people to hold seemingly contradictory viewpoints simultaneously, it teaches them to be comfortable with paradox, and in today's paradox-filled world that is a very useful lesson indeed.

Other benefits are more collective. To the extent that inclusivity encourages people to be more accepting of other's views, it creates a framework for dialogue and helps overcome our understandable, if unfortunate, tendency to seek comfort in the company of like-minded people and to shun those whose views make us uncomfortable.

A gathering of representatives of the local business community I attended several years ago illustrates how practicing inclusivity can create common ground in a polarized situation. The meeting had been called because a number of economic-development initiatives had been stymied by the environmental community. It was clear to the group that something different and maybe even conciliatory had to be tried. I was attending in a sort of ambassadorial role, as someone with environmentalist credentials who didn't have a knee-jerk hostility to business. I was soon singled out by a person I'll call Bill, who had plainly decided that since I was there as a spokesman for the environmentalists, I had to be one of the enemy. Fixing me with a baleful gaze, he proceeded to denounce the environmental movement for paying too much attention to trees while ignoring the real problem, which was the decay of our inner cities. And what was worse, he continued, the media wasn't paying any attention to this crisis, either!

Eventually his diatribe wound down and it was time for me to respond. I considered explaining why the environmental crisis was a crisis that could bring down all society, farms and forests and inner cities too. I considered saying nothing and clucking sympathetically. Instead I said, "Wait a minute, you think *you've* got a problem? You think the media won't pay any attention to *you*? I'm looking at the prospect of global ecosystem collapse, and the media won't cover *that*, either! The world's careering toward the abyss and all the media can pay attention to is Monica Lewinsky!"

I was saying, more or less, "I'm in the same boat as you!" It was an inclusive framework I had adopted, one that made room for his anger and mine too. And it worked. His expression softened and soon after he approached me as a reasonable fellow and potential friend.

It is important to note how broad and well, *inclusive* a concept inclusivity is. It's not only about other people's views. It can also be about their skin color or sexual orientation. It can be about ourselves, too: we can choose to be more or less open-minded about the various subpersonalities who live inside us. And finally, it is a stance we can adopt vis-à-vis abstract frameworks and ideas. If you were to ask me, "What does it mean to be integral?" three possible answers would occur to me. I could frame it in terms of Ken Wilber's "four quadrants." I could avail myself of Clare Graves's Spiral Dynamics model. Or, I could use the triad. As it happens, the latter course is the one I've taken, but that's because the triad is the framework that's closest to my heart, not because I believe that it's "right" and the others are "wrong," or that it's better than the others. I have chosen, in other words, to be inclusive in my attitude toward these frameworks. The integral way is like a pie that can be made with many different framework "flavors."

∽∽∽∽∽

Before moving on, let me take a moment to make the important point that practicing inclusivity does not require us to entirely abandon our capacity for discernment. Open-mindedness is a good thing, but critical intelligence is, too. We need to create value hierarchies for a very simple reason: there are better and worse things in the world. We need to be able to tell the difference between a well-made and a shabbily-made product, and we also need to be able to distinguish between insightful views and ones that are just plain dumb. And surely, to continue with this theme a moment longer, it is better to encourage our children to serve those in need than to commit genocide. Inclusivity does not require us to accord all our options equal treatment—that way lies the depth-dimension trap of absolute relativism. There is a paradox here (or perhaps it is better described as a subtle balancing act): among the things we must honor, as we practice inclusivity, are our intuitions about relative merit.

The Consequence: New Patterns of Organization

Once we have distanced ourselves from Viewpoint A to make room for Viewpoint B, in other words, once we have practiced inclusivity, the two viewpoints swirl around together in the more expansive space we have created for them, and out of this interaction something fundamentally new emerges.

If I am cooking chili, I mix together ketchup, Worcestershire sauce, chili powder, and other ingredients. If I taste the chili fresh out of the pot, it tastes one way. If I refrigerate the chili overnight, it tastes different. This is because the ingredients have blended and the whole has become tastier than the sum of its parts. Something new and integral has been created.

This is sometimes referred to as a "higher level" of organization because it "transcends and includes" its component parts.

We reorganize at this higher level when we allow different viewpoints to blend, so to speak, overnight.

This process is not limited to individuals. New patterns of organization can emerge in institutions and cultures, too. Or not, as the case may be. The year-2000 merger between oil giants Mobil and Exxon brought together two very different corporate cultures. According to Jeff Erikson, then a Mobil advisor, "I noticed early on the differences in the terminology that the two companies used. At Mobil, which was much more entrepreneurial, the talk tended to be about things like 'ownership' and 'empowerment.' At Exxon, where the management style was much more hierarchical and top-down, the operative word was 'execute.' The employees saw themselves as order-takers."[61]

According to Erikson, senior management hoped to forge a new culture out of the best that Mobil and Exxon had to offer. They wanted, in other words, an integral outcome—a fundamentally different pattern of organization. It didn't happen, though. Exxon was the bigger company and its culture simply took over. The new ExxonMobil was the same as the old Exxon, only bigger. Once things had settled down, says Erikson, "The broccoli had been salted, but it still tasted like broccoli."

This was an integral attempt that fell short. If this new pattern of organization does take hold, however, the transformative impact can be dramatic. We see the world in a profoundly different way. It's true that our values are different, but that's only part of it. Our *beings* are different, too. As a result, we are often graced with fresh insights into why things happen as they do. Our reality tunnel changes. And this is true whether the "we" in question is an individual, institution, or culture.

ॐॐॐॐ

At the individual level, reorganizing at this higher and more integral level can be useful in another way, too. It can form the basis of a self-sense—the sage—that supports meaningful engagement with the challenges we face locally and in the broader world.

Not that other personas don't provide a strong sense of public purpose—conservative Christians, for instance, are deeply committed to saving the souls of nonbelievers—but value systems like that fall short of the mark for many people. They feel too rigid and "either/or." What the times require is a new self-sense, a pattern of psychological organization that, like Christian fundamentalism, endows people with a sense of higher purpose and helps them maintain equanimity in the face of hardship, but that, unlike Christian fundamentalism, is a higher-level "yes/and" approach.

The integral way can do this. Because it is biased toward inclusivity, its tendency is to reach out and embrace, not push away. It is driven by the longing to take in *more*, to comprehend *more*, and ultimately to embody and represent the interests of *more*. It's not that people with integral "bones" are better than other people, it's that they are more inclined than your usual Joe or Joan to identify with other people, and with the natural world too. They're still looking after their own self-interest just like everyone else, but they experience self-interest differently, as something that extends beyond what the philosopher Alan Watts called their "skin-encapsulated egos." The inclusivity principle is relentless: it keeps asking us to take in more, to integrate more, ad infinitum. "Yes/and" is, in this sense, a path that takes us out to the edges of the universe. And this bias toward incorporating the other into one's field of caring shows up socially and politically as a predisposition to work for the good of all.

The integral way also helps people be more accepting of hard-to-swallow outcomes. This is because it teaches open-mindedness, and open-mindedness is the secular equivalent of faith. Where a devout Christian might respond to a distressing outcome by saying, "The Lord works in mysterious ways," the integrally inclined person might declare, "How can I be completely sure what is a 'right' or 'wrong' outcome?" It's basically the same answer—an answer born in humility—only without reference to a higher power. The integral way teaches equanimity, and that's very empowering. Equanimity is an antidote to despair, and that's a pearl beyond price during times like these.

The integral way thus inclines people to identify with the collective good, and it is also encouraging in the etymological sense of "giving courage to." These qualities make it an especially appropriate self-sense for our time. The integral way inspires civic engagement. The sage steps out of the shadows and tries to make a difference in the world.

The Benefit: Breakthrough Solutions

From out of this new pattern of organization, a host of good things flows. Some we have already identified. The integral way can deliver invaluable insights, as it did, for instance, in helping me better understand my relationship with my father. It can provide a useful framework for dialogue, as it did in my conversation with "Bill." It can supply straightforward strategic solutions, examples of which we will see in the next chapter. And finally, it can serve as the organizing principle for a self-sense that integrates the commitment to engage the world with a strong sense of personal responsibility and what my father called "moral vigor."

All these benefits have an objective aspect, that is, they all *solve problems*:

- *Integral insights* promote peace of mind—and peace between people too.
- *Integral dialogue* promotes understanding of self and others and helps overcome ignorance and mistrust.
- *Breakthrough strategies* solve problems, by definition.
- The *integral self-sense*, while its value is mostly intrinsic, also has instrumental value in that it helps us address a profound social problem—the fact that millions and maybe even billions of people around the world lack a deep sense of civic engagement.

What the integral way's "new pattern of organization"

really offers, in the end, is access to *breakthrough solutions*. And this is what makes the integral way so important. It offers a cornucopia of solutions to the problems of our time.

৵৵৵৵

What makes integral solutions so special? We can begin with the fact that they aren't "outside the box" so much as "higher-level." Instead of representing Viewpoint A in a face-off against Viewpoint B, the integral problem solver stands above both viewpoints and tries to integrate them, along with other relevant perspectives, into a seamless whole.

It's not quite correct to say that the game is no longer about winning, but it's not entirely off the mark, either. If the integral problem solver achieves her goal, she still prevails in the sense of getting her way, but now she has prevailed *on behalf of* the entire group, not *over* anyone. She has incorporated everyone's interests into her solution.

Integral problem solving is not quite the same as mediation, although there is some overlap. If Joe and Jane are divorcing, a skilled mediator might help them devise a financial settlement that leaves neither of them fuming. Useful though that service is, it isn't integral problem solving; it's facilitation. An even more skilled mediator might help the couple find ways to stay together, and do so feeling positive about each other and the future. This solution is more integral in nature. It is higher-level and comes closer to addressing the problem at its source; it gets at the deep structures underlying the issue. This is typical of integral solutions. There is an irony here, if only a semantic one: higher-level solutions, as a rule, cut deeper.

Integral solutions also tend to be quite bold, so much so that they often involve starting over. But we must take care to define our terms precisely here. Bolshevism involved starting over, but it wasn't integral. It threw out the old and tried to bring in something completely new, and it failed miserably. It was operating under the old "either/or" paradigm: you're either a capitalist or a communist, and the capitalists must go. The integral approach doesn't throw out the existing pieces, it reassembles them at a higher level. This is a fundamentally different approach to starting over.

Integral problem solving is thus both radical *and* conservative: radical because it gets at the root of the problem (the word "radical" is derived from the Latin *radix*, root), and conservative in the special sense that it *conserves* what came before—it "transcends and *includes*," it doesn't "transcend and *discard*."

The integral approach can seem foolhardy and even grandiose to people who are accustomed to small steps and cautious thinking. From the integral perspective, however, integral solutions are supremely logical. When the real problem is less the issue itself than the level at which the issue is being addressed, it only makes sense to raise the search to a higher level. This is the perspective that caused Albert Einstein to remark so famously, "You can't solve a problem at the same level that it was created. You have to rise above it to the next level."

At the end of the day, this is why the integral way has such enormous potential to drive positive change. It is easy to feel that we've reached a dead end and that there's no way out of our current dilemma. The integral approach provides an exit route. People may blink at the out-of-left-field originality of integral solutions, but they do not offend. They do not offend because they do not reject: they are inclusive and "conservative." Yet they are also radical, and it is this unlikely combination that provides grounds for hope. We need radical solutions because nothing less will do. Yet our solutions must also be conservative and inclusive, because only by taking that approach can they muster the broad buy-in that is required if there is to be any hope of achieving meaningful, rapid change.

For example, let's say we want to design a business ownership structure that effectively subordinates the pursuit of profits to the greater public good. That's a great idea—and one, as we shall see in the next chapter, that is being actively pursued—but it cannot possibly succeed unless there is a real reverence for what makes capitalist enterprise tick along with the commitment to transform it in important ways. A basic principle underlies all capitalism: if you take a financial risk, you can get rewarded for it—and the bigger the risk, the greater the prospective reward. Any transformative enterprise model that tries to eliminate this is doomed. It has the "radical" part down but is insufficiently "conservative." "Risk/return" is a game people like to play, and that's a desire—a fundamental human motivation, really—that can't be legislated or designed away.

Integral solutions are an odd duck and a rare bird, simultaneously radical and conservative, unlikely and achievable. And therein, quite precisely, lies their genius.

CHAPTER 9:
A CULTURAL EMERGENT

Beneath the Radar

In a world where it is very difficult to reach consensus on any-thing, most people seem to agree on this one thing: these are extraordinary times. The dominant mood is pessimistic, some-times even apocalyptic. But despite all the bad news and pre-vailing gloom, our situation is by no means hopeless. When a body is attacked by disease, it starts producing antibodies, and so it is with our body politic.

These antibodies take the form of new multilateral policies such as the Kyoto Protocol, which begins to address the cli-mate-change crisis, and the recently announced IMF commit-ment to allow impoverished countries to claim bankruptcy and renegotiate their debt obligations with lender nations.

They take the form of renewable-energy technologies such as wind (currently the world's fastest-growing energy technol-ogy), solar, and fuel cells.

They take the form of the growing ranks of citizen organi-zations, now a powerful force in global governance, that are speaking up loudly for the disenfranchised.

And finally, they take the form of the increasingly clear perception, on the part of billions of people around the world, that the current way of doing things simply isn't working, and that some fundamental breakthroughs in how we manage and distribute our resources will be required if we are to reverse our downward trajectory and set course toward what R. Buckmin-ster Fuller called "a world that works for 100 percent of human-ity...without ecological offense or the disadvantage of anyone."

Globally we are in a state of emergency. The word, as the psychologist Stanislaus Grof has noted, means two things. An "emergency" is a crisis, and it is also a process of emerging. Today's global emergency is producing "emergents" of every imaginable sort, ranging from new laws and policies to new technologies to new mindsets and values.

Some of these emergents have already made it into the media spotlight. Others are still beneath the radar, not because they are trivial but because the media work in mysterious ways. This is the status of the integral way. It is a largely unrecognized cultural emergent.

Here and There, but Not Yet Everywhere

There is a good reason for this, actually: the integral emergent is still very early-stage. It's not as if McDonald's is going to have to tear down its golden arches any time soon to make way for the integral juggernaut. Still, for those with eyes to see, integral initiatives are noticeably more prominent on the cultural landscape today than they were a few years ago. In fact, enough of these undertakings are underway for it to qualify as a trend.

If the great majority of people, media included, haven't spotted this yet, it's because the integral way is still, to a significant degree, an emergent without a name. "Yuppies" only became a cultural fixture after there was a word for them. Ditto for "hippies" and "eggheads." But who knows what "integral" means? Very few people at this stage, so integral initiatives tend to go unrecognized.

But they are here, they are proliferating, and they could even have a significant impact, in some cases a lot sooner than one might reasonably expect.

Café Conversations

On the morning of 9-11, shortly after the World Trade Center buildings had come tumbling down, I abandoned my television set and went out into the street. The hijacked planes had flown almost directly overhead; a sense of shock was in the air. By chance, I encountered a fellow who had recently done some contracting work for me. We come from very different worlds.

He is working class, blue-collar, and a Catholic with heaps of children. I am overeducated, childless, and agnostic.

We stood in silence for a moment. "It's unbelievable," I said eventually.

He nodded in agreement. "There is something terribly wrong with the world, isn't there?" he said.

His words echoed my thoughts precisely. In the past, I had shied away from conversations of any depth with this person because I assumed they would drive us apart. Quite the opposite had happened here. 9-11 had brought us together.

We were not alone. In the days and weeks following 9-11, traumatized Americans around the country turned to each other for support. In casual conversations and more structured gatherings, neighbors who had been ignoring or tolerating each other for years suddenly found themselves sharing their fears, confusion, grief, and rage.

The horrific terrorist attacks had had an unintended consequence. Before 9-11, people had hesitated to bring their private views into any public space that didn't feel safe. The breakdown in community was so far gone that it was only in gatherings of the obviously like-minded that people dared to speak up. Osama bin Laden and his band of not-so-merry men mended, if only briefly, the country's badly frayed social fabric. Ironically, their crime against humanity made our public spaces feel emotionally safe.

In addition to being physical places, public spaces are also containers for emotions. They can be joyous or downcast, trusting or dubious. The same is true for our more private social spaces, too. Every day, every hour, in bedrooms in the U.S. and around the world, lovers quarrel and then reunite because of swings in the weather of their shared space. Typically, one or both partners wants badly to say something, but doesn't dare. When he or she finally screws up the courage to speak up, this shifts the mood dramatically. If things go downhill, the conversation degenerates into mutual recrimination. But if things go well and the partners start sharing their feelings in an atmosphere of mutual support, something miraculous happens. The relationship that only minutes before felt impoverished and fragile suddenly feels rich, resilient, and back on track. And all because the lovers created a safe social space.

The triad can help us understand this dynamic. The depth dimension is where we store the secrets we feel we're not allowed to say. When we conceal something from a lover, it is often doubly painful because lovers come together to erase boundaries, not create them—the whole idea is to minimize the constraints on the flow of feelings. Their shared goal is to make the channel between the depth dimension and social domain as wide open as possible. When the dam finally breaks and the secret emotion—anger, betrayal, whatever—is brought into the social space, and if the process that results from that revelation is handled gracefully, the boundary between the depth dimension and social domain comes down and all becomes well again.

Whether the social space is in a bedroom or a town square, if silence reigns it is probably not a healthy place. Usually the silence comes from distrust, and distrust is corrosive whether it's a Saddam Hussein that's responsible or a democracy where discourse is in tatters.

Safe social spaces—or, if you prefer, spaces that are refreshed regularly and gently by the waters of the depth dimension—are vitally important. They keep marriages alive, and democracies too. They are the glue that maintains the social fabric. Unfortunately, in the U.S. of late, we've been doing a pretty wretched job of keeping our public spaces safe. It's one of the main things people have in mind when they bemoan the "breakdown of community."

How do you address this problem? You get people who would otherwise avoid each other engaging in dialogue in a space where they feel safe doing so, that's how—you restore communication between society and the depth dimension, in other words—and you get it to happen in many different venues. And that, it turns out, is precisely what some long-time members of the social-change community have set out to do.

Vicki Robin, coauthor with the late Joe Dominguez of the best-selling *Your Money or Your Life*, launched the first Conversation Café (www.conversationcafe.org) in mid-2001 out of "a conviction that social intelligence grows in the presence of people not like oneself. Engaging people with views different from one's own encourages self-reflection, and without self-reflection no system can transform."[62] The facilitated ninety-minute gatherings are held in public spaces like cafés, and they are open to everyone—they're not just for the like-minded. Participants are encouraged to listen closely and not try to "win."

Although progressives are the most natural constituency for the dialogues, Robin and her associates have managed to attract a diverse group of participants. "The media have been our greatest ally in this," she says, while also citing various guerrilla strategies—posters, community calendars, and the like.

The conversations are a success, if their proliferation is any indication. At last count there were more than twenty Conversation Cafés in Seattle, and they had been launched in about a dozen other cities as well.

There is also the World Café (www.theworldcafe.com), which was founded by a group that includes organizational-learning experts Juanita Brown and David Isaacs. Like its Conversation Café counterpart, the World Café website features a statement adapted from cultural critic William Greider: "Creating a positive future begins in human conversation. The simplest and most powerful investment any member of a community or an organization may make in renewal is to begin talking with other people as though the answers mattered."[63] In a World Café dialogue, groups of four to five people explore questions that really matter to their life, work, or community. People cross-pollinate ideas between tables in several rounds of conversation, keeping a record of their emerging insights on the Café tablecloths. As people connect their discoveries, collective knowledge grows, a sense of the larger whole emerges, the wisdom of the group becomes more visible, and opportunities for action are revealed. Tens of thousands of people on five continents have participated in World Café conversations focusing on key organizational and community issues in settings ranging from crowded hotel ballrooms with 1,200 people in attendance to cozy living rooms.

And then there is the Commons Café, founded by social activist Sharif Abdullah. Its goal is to bring together "people who do not previously know each other" and "who are different from each other in some fundamental ways (race/ethnicity, culture, class, ideology)."[64] Abdullah wants to "connect people who would not otherwise be connected, to dissolve the barriers that separate us."[65]

Here we have three related collaborative-dialogue initiatives sprouting up independently on the cultural landscape. Quite a coincidence, no? But of course it's not a coincidence at all. Something is happening here, as Bob Dylan said back in his salad days, and what's happening is a cultural emergent, and an *integral* cultural emergent at that. It's integral because all three types of café conversation are attempting to create *inclusive* public spaces, and inclusivity, as we have seen, is the first principle of integral thinking. Café conversations set out to create a space that's big enough to include lots of different views, on the principle that if you do it in a way that promotes thoughtful discussion, all kinds of good things can happen. Vicki Robin puts it this way: "Perhaps, in the process of listening and conversing, we'll open our minds a bit. Maybe even change them."[66]

Open-mindedness: now there's another integral attribute. In the end, that's what café conversations are: training grounds in open-mindedness. Boot camps at Parris Island teach young men to be Marines; café conversations teach citizens to be integral. The integral approach is a whole lot gentler, to be sure. Café conversations create a supportive setting and stop there: there aren't any drill sergeants hollering at you to give him fifty push-ups. In both cases, however, the goal is the same—consciousness change at the individual level with a corresponding shift in social capital.

In another sense, the two types of training are wildly different, of course. Boot camps inculcate obedience; conversation
cafés teach self-reflection. Or, to frame the same thought in the
language of the triad, boot camps teach you to suppress the
depth dimension and salute society; dialogue supports you to
infuse (and strengthen) society with your depth-dimension
authenticity. Where boot camps grind you down so a new,
superdutiful self can emerge, café conversations are transport
devices, ladders leading up to the integral way.

The Fourth Sector

Today, three broadly defined institutional sectors have primary responsibility for overseeing our communal affairs—government (the public sector), business (the private sector), and
nonprofit organizations (the social sector, also known as "civil
society" organizations). These sectors lend themselves to being
categorized by domain:

- Corporations are your quintessential objective-
  domain institution: they are all about strategy, all
  about achieving objectives, which are almost invari-
  ably couched in terms of profits.

- The public sector—government—sustains the structures of society by enforcing its laws and defending
  its borders.

- The function of many, though not all, civil society
  organizations is to look after the underserved, to give
  voice to the voiceless. While there are a great many
  hobbyist civil society organizations without a service
  agenda, there are also innumerable organizations
  whose mission it is to care for the poor or protect the
  environment. These civil society organizations represent the depth dimension at the governance table, and
  over the last few decades their numbers have risen
  dramatically. According to one estimate, there are
  currently well over 40,000 international civil society
  organizations in operation, up from under 10,000 in
  1978.[67] And literally millions of civil society organiza-

tions, a great many of them with unambiguous social and environmental agendas, now operate locally.

Given how neatly the three sectors slot into the triad, one might hope that they could collectively govern well and wisely. Unfortunately, they have shown themselves to be ill-equipped, both individually and collectively, to meet the governance challenges of our time. They all have a "legacy problem," a term from the computer industry for the headaches that come from having to build new software systems on top of old ones. Ever wonder why Windows can get so moody? It's the legacy problem: Windows XP rides on top of, hang onto your Pentium, that prehistoric artifact, DOS.

Business, government, and nonprofits came into being during dramatically different times from those that obtain today. For all three sectors, things like economic globalization, resource scarcity, environmental decline, the victory of free-market capitalism, and rapid technological advances have dramatically changed the rules of the game.

Corporations are coming under increasing pressure to take an active role in helping to address the world's problems. They are expected to cross over, so to speak, from the objective domain to society. This requires them to integrate the public good into their business decisions, and this is something they weren't designed for.

Governments are having to adapt to new circumstances, too. To begin with, they're not the kingpins they once were. Globalization has reduced the influence of individual nation-states, which are increasingly being forced to share power with corporations and civil society. And the public sector must deal with a second problem, too. Bureaucracy has long been a hall-mark of the public sector, and today it is more burdensome than ever. Like never before, the race goes to the swift nowadays—it goes to the objective-domain institutions that excel at going fast, faster, fastest—and social-domain governments are notoriously slow.

The depth dimension-based, nonprofit social sector has a

legacy problem, too. Historically, it has depended on contributions from private donors and foundations. That's nice work if you can get it, but it has also produced a sector characterized by institutional passivity and a striking dearth of entrepreneurial capacity. That's passé. Handouts are out these days; the entrepreneurial spirit reigns supreme. The social sector is under considerable pressure to get with it and start showing that it can be as quick on its feet as the most agile business start-up. This requires a skill set—an objective orientation—that's vastly different from what was required during the old grant-and-donation days.

In sum, businesses are increasingly expected to be more committed to the public good—in other words, to act more like the public and social sectors—while government and nonprofits are expected to be leaner and meaner and more entrepreneurial—more like the private sector. What this adds up to is an emerging demand for a fundamentally new sort of institution that is sustained by profits yet committed to serving humanity—that, in other words, reconciles the traditional tension between private enterprise and the public good. When all is said and done, these "social purpose" or "for benefit" institutions comprise an entirely new governance sector—a "fourth sector." And it is a sector, it must be added, that is deeply integral in nature: it includes the best features of the public, private, and social sectors; it constitutes a fundamentally new pattern of organization; and it offers a potentially powerful breakthrough solution to the fact that our current governance sectors are all anachronistic.

A simple two-by-two matrix can help us understand the larger trend that is unfolding. The matrix's X axis focuses on the enterprise's purpose. It establishes a continuum running from "maximizes benefit to owners" on the left to "maximizes social benefit" on the right. The Y axis addresses how the enterprise generates its income, and runs from "earns its revenue by selling goods and/or services" at the top to "collects its revenue through taxes or donations" at the bottom.

When we plug business, government, and civil society into this matrix, we find that the private sector lands in the upper-left quadrant (*earns* income to *maximize benefit for owners*), while the public and social sectors are situated in the lower-right quadrant (*collects* income through taxes or donations to *maximize social benefit*). We are now culturally laboring to give birth to a sector whose center of gravity is in the upper-right quadrant (*earns* income to *maximize social benefit*).

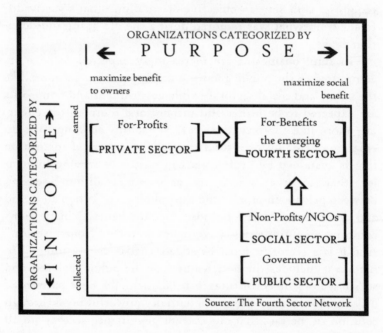

ORGANIZATIONS CATEGORIZED BY

← P U R P O S E →

maximize benefit to owners

maximize social benefit

ORGANIZATIONS CATEGORIZED BY

↑ I N C O M E ↓

earned

collected

For-Profits
PRIVATE SECTOR

For-Benefits
the emerging
FOURTH SECTOR

Non-Profits/NGOs
SOCIAL SECTOR

Government
PUBLIC SECTOR

Source: The Fourth Sector Network

At the risk of imposing a degree of order that isn't warranted by the organic and inherently unruly nature of this cultural emergent, we can group the attempts to birth this fourth sector into three broad categories. First, in recent years, there has been a marked upsurge in efforts by social-change advocates to coax the private, public, and social sectors in the direction of the upper-right quadrant, where social benefit is maximized and income is earned:

- "Socially responsible business," "sustainable business," and "cause-related marketing" are among the many initiatives intended to make the business sector more socially and environmentally conscious.

- "Lean government," a movement championed during the Clinton Administration by then-Vice President Gore, attempts to make the public sector more like business, while the increasingly fashionable policy of privatization takes this impulse to its logical limit. Rather than try to remake government in the image of business, privatization takes the bull by the free-market horns and straightforwardly shifts public-sector functions to the private sector.

- The social sector, too, is awash with initiatives to make institutions more innovative and entrepreneurial. The emerging emphasis on "measurable results" calls for nonprofits to quantify their performance the same way businesses do, and more and more foundations are tying transition to economic sustainability by their grantees into their funding strategies. These are only two of the many ways in which social-sector institutions are being encouraged to act like businesses and earn their keep rather than collect it from friends and foundations.

Unfortunately, the boundaries of these three sectors can be stretched only so far. The track record of recent decades has delivered a double message. First, these sectors *do* have a certain amount of "give." Second, at the end of the day, darn it all, they're pretty inelastic. Legal, capital, and other constraints restrict how much change is possible. For instance, the requirement that public corporations maximize return to shareholders keeps management from pursuing many socially responsible initiatives, while nonprofit organizations that start to earn a portion of their income through market activity often find traditional sources of funding drying up because they are now perceived as more financially self-sufficient and therefore less needy than their counterparts.

The second front in the effort to create a vital fourth sector is bolder: instead of trying to tweak sectoral boundaries—challenge enough, to be sure!—flat-out break the mold instead. An organization called The ManyOne Network provides an example of this. A start-up, subscription-based Internet portal service provider operating in the same general market space as AOL and MSN, but with a breakthrough browser and too many other technical and service innovations to mention, ManyOne is a for-profit enterprise with a difference. It accepts investment capital, but offers a capped, not open-ended, return. One hundred percent ownership in ManyOne is being vested in a non-profit foundation, The ManyOne Foundation, whose board of directors will consist of prominent members of the social-change community. Because of this, it is a virtual certainty that the company will never go public or be sold to a commercial entity. Gross profits earned by The ManyOne Network will go to the Foundation, which in turn will distribute those profits to organizations and enterprises whose activities are aligned with the Earth Charter, a landmark document that sets out the principles underlying a just and environmentally sustainable society. As for investors, their capped equity interest is being converted to debt, which will be repaid over time out of gross profits.

ManyOne's innovative ownership and governance structure attempts to harness the genius of the marketplace in service to the greater good. If it succeeds, ManyOne will have provided proof-of-concept for a model that can be replicated by thousands upon thousands of social entrepreneurs around the world. And what makes this model especially important is that it embeds the commitment to the public good in the institutional DNA. Many socially responsible companies currently commit a percentage of profits to social or environmental causes, and while this is admirable, it is also optional: management can change its mind at any time. ManyOne's overriding commitment to the public good is not discretionary.[68]

These on-the-ground activities notwithstanding, it must be

remembered that the fourth sector is a purely theoretical construct. It is entirely possible to create an enterprise with striking fourth sector characteristics without defining it as such—and that, in fact, is precisely what the ManyOne team did. As is usually the case, the cultural emergent has preceded the attempt to define it.

There is considerable value in naming an emergent, though, even if it does come after the fact. It shines a light for people on the cultural ecosystem in which they are participating, and this grounds and empowers them. This is where the third and still-embryonic type of effort is focused—on providing a framework that will help the people who are driving the emergence of the fourth sector better understand the stream they are swimming in, and in the process, make it easier for them to fashion the infrastructure and replicable models upon which long-term success depends.

In 1999, a cross-sectoral, cross-disciplinary network of individuals and organizations was formed for the express purpose of doing this. Dubbed the Fourth Sector Network, it describes its role as follows:

> A critical mass of organizations is gathering within, or transitioning toward, the emerging Fourth Sector. But this activity is sustained mostly by the support infrastructure of the public, private, and social sectors. In order for Fourth Sector organizations to thrive and grow, there is a clear need to develop a supportive ecosystem that is tailored particularly to their needs.
>
> The development of such an ecosystem can be best catalyzed through the formation of a network infrastructure that:
>
> - distinguishes and connects the fragmented activity that is currently taking place in the emerging Fourth Sector,
>
> - advances a coherent "operating system" that enables organizations that support Fourth Sector activity to leverage and coordinate their efforts, and

- *facilitates effective engagement and connection between Fourth Sector organizations and their stakeholders (especially those from other sectors).*

The Fourth Sector Network has been formed to catalyze the development of this supportive ecosystem.[69]

The ultimate Fourth Sector institution would do more than align private wealth creation with the public good. It would also operate transparently, be governed democratically, aim to eliminate social and environmental harm, and do lots of other really cool stuff, too. And indeed there are efforts underway to create these ultimate institutions. For the most part, however, the exigencies of building a business are mandating a measure of compromise. Still, the overall trajectory is unmistakable: slowly but surely, we are witnessing the emergence of a fourth sector.

The New America Foundation

If a powerful fourth sector is created, it will be because a bunch of creative, committed individuals make it happen, not because it generates a groundswell of support among mainstream institutions. If the notion of creating a new, fourth sector seems a bit fanciful, and it is understandable if it does, the idea of a mainstream mainstay like Microsoft going fourth sector seems even more so. Some aspects of the integral emergent are outsider activities, by definition.

Not all of them, though. The integral emergent is also getting traction inside the Beltway, not your basic hotbed of outsider agitation. The New America Foundation, which opened its doors on Connecticut Avenue in the nation's capital in 1999, is showing the way here. Its target isn't consciousness change or sectoral reform, it's the American political system. The think tank relies on what it calls "a venture capital approach" to invest in "outstanding individuals and policy ideas that transcend the conventional political spectrum."[70] The policies it espouses are neither conventionally liberal nor conventionally conservative, neither Democratic nor Republican. They are integral.

As with many other aspects of the integral emergent, the solutions offered by the New America Foundation emerge from the perception that our dominant ideologies and institutions aren't equipped to meet the challenges of our time. In *The Radical Center*, CEO Ted Halstead and senior fellow Michael Lind write, "To us, it seems obvious that the familiar varieties of liberalism and conservatism, developed as they were in response to the Second Industrial Revolution, are largely irrelevant in the fundamentally different environment of the first half of the twenty-first century."[71]

The perspective set forth in *The Radical Center* is "radical/conservative," another hallmark of the integral way. Explicitly so, in fact. Halstead and Lind write, "We use the word *radical*...to emphasize that we are interested not in tinkering at the margin of our inherited public, private and communal institutions but rather in promoting, when necessary, a wholesale revamping of their component parts."[72]

In this statement, they are straightforwardly laying claim to their radical pedigree, but buried in this assertion is a very conservative assumption—that radical actions consist of "revamping...component parts," in other words, "*conserving*." Elsewhere Halstead and Lind directly stake their claim to the "conservative" label:

> [I]t is reformers [like us] rather than reactionaries who have a better claim to the label of conservative. Who are more conservative—those who would sacrifice the part to save the whole, or those who would prefer to lose the whole rather than alter it in any way? The true patriots in American history have always understood that when conditions change it is necessary to pursue perennial goals by new means. Renovation is conservation by means of innovation.[73]

Their approach is also *inclusive*. "Our political process tends to dichotomize issues," Halstead says. "For instance, there's a recurring tension between the principles of fairness and flexibility. In areas such as school choice and social security, Republicans opt for flexibility, while Democrats say this is unfair. The challenge is to break free of the either/or framework. We need to find solutions that allow for both fairness *and* flexibility."[74]

Halstead's bias toward inclusivity extends to his embrace of what he and Lind define as the three bedrock values of American culture—liberty, equality, and communal solidarity (essentially the liberty, fraternity, and equality of the French revolution). They write:

> Some argue that the central value of the American tradition is liberty; others, equality; still others, communal solidarity. These schools of thought are all partially correct, but ultimately wrong. The perennial American tradition cannot be defined in terms of any single value. Rather, it consists of a complex of values—values that are complementary, not contradictory. The more accurate formulation would therefore be liberty and equality and community—each in its appropriate sphere.[75]

In combination, this dissatisfaction with mainstream institutions and embrace of radical/conservative inclusivity results in a *new pattern of organization*—the authors' "radical center"—along with *breakthrough solutions*, in fact scads of them: the book devotes page upon page to proposals for reinventing health care, social security, our tax and electoral systems, and more.

In one of Halstead and Lind's radical/conservative policy proposals, they address the increasing tension between the need for modern-day enterprises to operate in a lean and highly adaptive mode, versus the need for employees to have long-term financial security.

> The central challenge of a new Information Age social contract is to destroy less-productive jobs and less-productive businesses, without destroying lives and livelihoods. There are two sides to this challenge: the need of America's employ-

ees for greater security in the new economy, and the need of America's employers for greater flexibility in the new economy. A failure to meet either side of this challenge will ultimately hurt all parties involved. That is, if reliable and flexible safety net programs do not make it easy for workers to move from one job to another or one sector to another, without devastating losses in income or gaps in insurance coverage, then voters will pressure politicians to preserve outmoded jobs and antiquated industries, thereby threatening the very engine of prosperity. Likewise, if our social contract does not afford modern corporations the increased speed and flexibility they so need in the new economy, then our engine of prosperity will suffer just as seriously.[76]

Historically, these two needs have been viewed as irreconcilable, with the political right arguing that it is more important to give business a free hand, and the political left siding with the social safety net. For Halstead and Lind, this is a needless debate. They believe we can have our economic competitiveness, and our safety net, too. The key is to "sever the traditional link between the provision of benefits and employers (though not employment). The guiding principle of an Information Age social contract should be to link all benefits directly to individuals rather than to employers or to other intermediary institutions."[77]

From this starting point, Halstead and Lind proceed to lay out the outlines of what they describe as "a new, citizen-based social contract that pairs mandatory personal insurance for health care and mandatory personal retirement savings with guaranteed government safety nets, thereby creating a flexible new workforce able to enjoy the freedoms of today's contingent workers and the security of today's full-time employees, while simultaneously freeing American companies from the unnecessary burdens of benefit administration."[78]

This approach, like the others Halstead and Lind propose, would be both radical and conservative: radical because it cuts boldly to the root of the problem, and conservative because it preserves employer flexibility and employee security, both of which are threatened by the current, uncontrolled course of events.

In developing policies that do not slot easily into left or right pigeonholes, Ted Halstead believes he and his colleagues are articulating an emerging mandate. "More people now self-identify as independents than as Republicans or Democrats," he says. "People are looking for something altogether better and fundamentally different."[79]

The New America Foundation is scoring big points in the public-policy community. The organization has teamed with *The Atlantic Monthly* to publish an annual "State of the Union" issue, which appears shortly before the presidential address on the same subject. *The Radical Center* features back-page blurbs from two prominent politicians. "A political manifesto worthy of the Information Age," proclaims Arizona Senator John McCain (duly noted as "Republican"), while the book "is much more than the future of American politics—it's the future of America," according to Senator John Breaux of Louisiana ("Democrat"). In 2001, the *Washington Post* ran a lengthy profile of Halstead with the headline, "*Big Thinker: Ted Halstead's New America Foundation Has It All—Money, Brains and Buzz.*" Since its inception, the foundation has published more articles in the *Los Angeles Times* and the *New York Times* than any other think tank in the country, according to Halstead. "It's because we're offering a fundamentally new model," he says. "We're a sort of public-policy home for the homeless."

It is doing well financially, too. Its annual budget of about $3 million makes it "bigger than all but the very largest think tanks, and the budget is growing," says Halstead.

It must be said that Halstead and Lind's viewpoints are a bit untypical as far as integral perspectives go. Integral thinkers often view themselves as outsiders; Halstead and Lind are working from inside the system. Integral thinkers are also often intent on integrating *inner* and *outer*. They want, in other words, to unite the inner world of consciousness change with the outer world of social and political transformation. It's an understandable desire, if you think about it: if your impulse is to integrate stuff, why not try to integrate *everything*? If their book is any measure, however, Halstead and Lind are focused exclusively on the outer: topics like consciousness change and personal development go unmentioned.

This isn't to suggest that they discount the depth dimension entirely. As we have seen, the depth dimension is home to critically important cultural "secrets" that don't get the public attention they deserve. Halstead and Lind are committed to integrating these issues into our policy conversations and decisions. Indeed, it is what drives them. Before launching the New America Foundation, Halstead founded and headed up Redefining Progress, the nonprofit that developed the Genuine Progress Indicator (GPI), an alternative to the Gross Domestic Product (GDP) that was discussed in Chapter 7. As I noted, the GPI measures if we're really doing well or badly as a society, rather than how we seem to be doing based on the often misleading data in the GDP. It was Halstead's way to integrate the negative aspects of our culture—our "secrets"—into the economic pronouncements that shape our national mood and policies.

Halstead and Lind's integrative "radical conservatism" has an intensely strategic orientation and little or no regard for the inner, psychological dimension of the integral way. Yet it is integral anyway. Their approach is *inclusive*, this approach produces a *new pattern of organization*, and this in turn produces *breakthrough solutions*. Halstead, Lind, and their New America Foundation colleagues are integral wolves in policy-wonk clothing. And they're carving out a niche for themselves in the nation's capital.

Looking Ahead

Will integral initiatives like these continue to blossom? I suspect they will, largely because we badly need breakthrough solutions and the integral way supplies them. Every culture, ours included, has its own genius, by which I mean two things: an enormous capacity for breakthrough creativity, and also (and this is the original meaning of "genius") a guardian spirit or deity that looks after its best interests (as in "genie"). That is what the integral way is—an emerging, inchoate but irrepressible expression of our culture's genius.

For evidence that this is so, I turn to the New England Conservatory, one of the country's leading music institutions. In recent years it has transformed its mission, such that its focus is no longer on graduating trained musicians, but on preparing students to be teachers and scholars as well as artists. If we think back to the triad, we can see that the curriculum has been expanded so that it now teaches excellence in all three domains: scholarship (the objective domain), teaching (society), and the arts (the depth dimension and objective domain in combination).

Why the shift to this vastly more integral perspective? According to Eric Booth, a nationally known expert in arts and education, it arose out of the perception that "these were the skills that would be required of twenty-first-century musicians." Booth sees reason for hope in this: "If the classical music world, which reveres the established order in the most hidebound sort of way, can expand its vision as dramatically and radically as this, it can happen anywhere."[80]

Integral thinking isn't just for risk-takers, in other words, not just for wild-and-crazy visionaries. It's for anyone and everyone who hears the song of the twenty-first century and wants to respond appropriately. Is the integral way the next really big thing? That's impossible to say. But if the New England Conservatory and the many other signs of emergence are any indication, it's definitely here to stay.

CHAPTER 10:
A PATH PERSONAL AND POLITICAL

In the last chapter, we examined the integral way as the driver of much-needed social change. Our focus was primarily institutional. Here, we get personal. The integral way is not a passive concept, something that "gets done" in the world. It is something that you and I actively do; it is a practice, a way of being in the world. But what does this actually mean? What dimensions of experience must one remain alert to? How does one practice "deep strategy"—the art of engaging strategic issues at their deep-structural level? And how does one "engage the sage"—activate one's higher-level, integral identity? These are the questions we take up now.

Confronting the Dark Enchantment

Confusion—the labyrinth—is nothing new. The dark enchantment, the spell we fall under through long-term exposure to the tyranny of the objective, has been with us since time immemorial. But something very basic about that shadow has changed in recent years. Awakening from the dark enchantment used to be an exclusively interior challenge. Seeking to be free of our confusion, we journeyed into our depth dimension, sometimes by pursuing conscious spiritual practices such as meditation, and sometimes by being shipped out on the psychological roller-coaster ride that has come to be known as the hero's journey. Myths often projected this quest onto the outer world—Ulysses sailed the Aegean, Parsifal searched for the Grail, Theseus slew the Minotaur in Crete—but the actual landscape was the self. Those spells, labyrinths, and wastelands were all interior.

Today the wasteland still has that same inner dimension, but over the last few decades it has developed a second identity as well. The wasteland we are creating is now literal as well as metaphorical. The dam has broken and inner has surged into outer. Our psychological and spiritual confusion is wreaking havoc on the external world.

The reason for this can be explained in a single word: *scale*. With six billion people inhabiting the planet, and nine billion anticipated by mid-century, our species has become a geological force, as powerful in its way as hurricanes and volcanoes. One person out of balance is bad news for what was once quaintly referred to as his or her "immortal soul." A million people out of balance may produce unfortunate results for a local ecosystem. Six billion people out of balance, and climbing, tear apart the world.

We have reached an unprecedented point in history, one in which subjective, interior myth and empirical, external reality have finally merged. For millennia, people blamed themselves for floods, droughts, and the like. If only they had not failed morally, if only they had made the proper sacrifices, the gods would not be punishing them. Every new spring was a miracle, a gift the gods could have chosen to withhold.

This was magical thinking, and misguided. But now it *is* in fact our own behavior that is releasing the demons of pollution and climate change. Dying lakes and oceans, drought, floods, fires—these are all our doing. More than a few informed observers believe that the survival of our species is at stake.[81]

The wasteland was problem enough when it was strictly interior. Now that it has cast its shadow over the future of life on this planet, it has fundamentally altered the moral context for the choices we make during our lives. Like never before, our spiritual pursuits must have a political dimension, and our political commitment must be more than casual. It is no longer enough to travel the interior realms in search of self-actualization and the experience of what we might call "deep meaning": the times demand "deep responsibility," too. The need for civic engagement has been raised to a new and global level.

I am not suggesting that the integral way requires everyone to take to the streets, although I am not advising against it. Nor am I suggesting that it requires everyone to become a full-time sustainability activist, although here, too, I wouldn't object. What is required, rather, is focused attention. The dark enchantment is insidious, and it is pervasive. The integral way requires us to be constantly on the lookout for its presence, both in ourselves and in our culture, and to work steadfastly to combat it. In addition to society-based "deep responsibility," there must be depth-dimension "deep awareness," too.

The actual steps we take need not be dramatic. It might be a matter of speaking up when we previously would have remained silent, or pulling a different lever in the voting booth, or trying a different approach with our children. The whole world's a stage, not just the streets and barricades.

The integral way is underpinned by an admonition: *Stay alert. Keep your eyes open. Do not fall prey to the dark enchantment.* Once that becomes a habit, your heart and voice will follow.

Needless to say, we must be effective as well as attentive and responsible. There is a third blank to be filled in, in other words, and it occupies the objective domain. In what ways can we best transform our "deep responsibility" and "deep awareness" into effective action? The answer is: by practicing "deep strategy."

Practicing Deep Strategy

The Importance of Being Integral

Language reveals what we pay attention to, and what we disregard as well. The language of love is surprisingly impoverished: we have erotic love, mother love, and platonic love, but it is surprising that we don't have a much more comprehensive set of descriptors, considering love's place in our lives. The language of strategy is somewhat impoverished, too. The usual distinction we make is between tactics and strategy, and while this has merit—tactics are the steps we take to implement a higher-level strategic plan—it is also inadequate. At a minimum, there are two kinds of strategy, which we can think of as "shallow" and "deep." Whereas shallow strategies address symptoms, deep strategy attempts to get at the causes underlying them. Deep strategists take a system view of things and assume that if you want to correct system dysfunctionalities, you have to get at the root of the problem. If the dysfunctional system in question is an alcoholic family, you've got to get the alcoholic to change his or her ways, otherwise nothing positive of consequence can happen. The same principle applies to all dysfunctional systems: unless you address the underlying structures, any changes will be largely cosmetic. Deep strategies are by definition radical—you will recall that "radical" derives from the Latin *radix*, root—but they are also conservative: their goal is to restore, at a fundamental level, the vitality of the whole.

A true story from the Rocky Mountain Institute website (www.rmi.org) can help us better understand the difference between deep and shallow strategizing:

> In the early 1950s, the Dayak people of Borneo suffered from malaria. The World Health Organization had a solution: it sprayed large amounts of DDT to kill the mosquitoes that carried the malaria. The mosquitoes died; the malaria declined; so far, so good. But there were side effects. Among the first was that the roofs of people's houses began to fall down on their heads. It seemed that the DDT was also killing a parasitic wasp that had previously controlled thatch-eating caterpillars. Worse, the DDT-poisoned insects were eaten by geckos, which were eaten by cats. The cats started to die, the rats flourished, and the people were threatened by potential outbreaks of typhus and plague. To cope with these problems, which it had itself created, the World Health Organization was obliged to parachute 14,000 live cats into Borneo.
>
> The true story of Operation Cat Drop—now nearly forgotten at WHO—illustrates that if you don't know how things are interconnected, then often the cause of problems is solutions. On the other hand, if you understand the hidden connections between energy, climate, water, agriculture,

transportation, security, commerce, and economic and social development, then you can often devise a solution to one problem (such as energy) that will also create solutions to many other problems at no extra cost.[82]

In addition to being system-oriented, deep strategy is also deeply integral. As we saw in Chapter 8, the integral way takes us from *inclusivity* to a *new pattern of organization* to *breakthrough solutions*. This is also the path deep strategy takes. It is, to begin with, inclusive. Inclusivity runs vertically as well as horizontally: vertically, deep strategy includes the deep-structural level that conventional strategizing so often overlooks; horizontally, it takes special pains to treat the citizen, the seeker, and the strategist equally.

This inclusive approach produces, if not quite a new pattern of organization, a new self-sense that is virtually the same thing. It does so, in part, by supporting us to reinterpret terms whose meaning we thought we knew. As our understanding of the words we use to define ourselves changes, so does our sense of who we are. Consider, for instance, the word *excellence.* In corporations, it is usually thought of in exclusively objective terms, as a technical proficiency that enables us to achieve our goals efficiently. Deep strategy revises that understanding by transforming "excellence" into something integral and three-dimensional. In addition to its objective aspect, it gains a social identity—reliability and trustworthiness as a fellow citizen—and a depth dimension aspect too—the subjective experience of excellence, knowing you're doing the very best you can. For a corporation to qualify as "excellent," it must now deliver on all three fronts, not just the usual, technical one.

Or take the word "leadership." Again, the corporate context is revealing. In business culture, leadership is usually quite narrowly defined. Company X is an "industry leader" or a "technological leader." But is that really how we should be defining leadership? Shouldn't leadership have moral and even visionary attributes as well? Can a person or organization be a leader when the net effect of what they do, when all is said and done, aggravates the sustainability crisis and pushes us that much closer to disaster? Deep strategy takes us to these questions. It challenges us to insist on a definition of leadership that is calibrated to the actual requirements of our time.

Once we have this new self-sense, the result is often breakthrough solutions. Approaches that could never have been conceived through conventional strategizing virtually leap up and declare themselves, so obvious do they seem. This is because deep strategy takes us into territory that would otherwise have been ignored. The meanings we impute to words define our boundaries: when we expand our understanding of words like "excellence" and "leadership," the frontiers for strategic exploration open up, too.

Deep strategy is integral in yet another sense as well. It obliges people who pursue it to release their identification with the three domains, if only for the duration of the exercise. Deep strategy can only be practiced from a higher-level space where the agreed-upon goal is to overcome the realm wars that keep the strategist, the citizen, and the seeker at odds with each other. Deep strategy requires disidentification. It is, in this sense, the purview of the sage, the higher-level self who practices the integral way.

࿆࿆࿆࿆

In its basic contours, deep strategy is quite similar to conventional strategizing. One begins with a *presenting problem*—an issue that needs to be addressed. The next step is *diagnosis*, an analysis of the problem in the context of the underlying deep-structural dynamics (an important point of differentiation from conventional strategizing). The triad can help us do this, as can other integral frameworks. From there we proceed to *inquiry*, which takes the form of the following question (and here is another place where deep strategy differs from the usual approach): *In what ways can we resolve this problem, such that the needs of the strategist, citizen, and seeker are honored more or less equally?* Once a list of possible answers to this question has been developed, we proceed to *evaluation*. We assess the various options for their efficacy, feasibility, risks, and so on. From there we make our *choice* and, in theory, follow with *implementation*.

But not always. Deep strategizing tends to produce bold solutions, and boldness is not for everyone. Even if the recommendations generated by deep strategizing are never actually implemented, it can be a useful exercise, though. It frames strategic options in provocative new ways, it creates fresh understandings, and it stimulates dialogue. All this has intrinsic merit; all this refreshes the flow of discourse. In so doing, it supports organizational health, and that is true whether the "organization" in question is a corporation, a community, a family, or a single individual. Deep strategy thus serves a double purpose: it produces breakthrough solutions, and it provides a framework for dialogue.

Calling Big Daddy

We're in a strategic planning session at a multinational corporation. It could be Starbucks, Nike, McDonald's, Ford, BP, Citicorp, or any of a hundred other companies. It's a fictional enterprise, though—"Big Idea, Inc," which is the world's leading corporate proponent of deep strategy. The company's key executives are all conversant in the triad, and they have gathered for this meeting. The subject is a very vexing problem: the low esteem in which Big Idea and other global corporations are held, and what to do about it.

The company's Senior Vice President for Communication launches the discussion by telling her colleagues that public distrust of corporations is hovering near all-time highs. She quotes a 2002 *USA Today* article: "[T]rust in Corporate America is in shambles.... In the past nine months, the percentage of Americans who see Big Business as an actual threat to the nation's future has nearly doubled, to 38%."[83] She cites a landmark 2000 *Business Week* survey, in which 72 percent of respondents agreed that "business has gained too much power over too many aspects of American life," while 74 percent believed that corporations did a "poor" or "only fair" job of "being straightforward and honest in their dealings with consumers and employees."[84] She quotes from *Business Week*'s cover story: "[C]itizens feel uneasy about Big Business. The growing political issue is one that companies ignore at their peril."[85]

In addition to all this passive resentment, the Senior Vice President continues, there is considerable active resistance in the form of the worldwide antiglobalization movement, which has spawned massive demonstrations in Seattle, Prague, Washington, D.C., and elsewhere. A boycott of ExxonMobil, widely viewed as the chief corporate architect behind the campaign to delay action on climate change, built up enough momentum to compel the company to issue a statement that its business hadn't been affected, no, really, not at all. Now growing global anti-Americanism was beginning to make its mark as well, with a new venture called Mecca Cola threatening to take a sizable chunk of business away from Coca-Cola in Muslim countries.

There is also cause for concern on the judicial front, the Senior Vice President notes, where there has been a marked increase in attempts to hold companies, and in some cases entire industries, liable for the indirect consequences of their actions. Inspired by the enormous damages imposed on Big Tobacco, lawyers and citizen activists are targeting other industries as well. In the United States, the gun industry has come, so to speak, under the gun, with some thirty lawsuits filed by various agencies and organizations. State and local governments have sued paint manufacturers, maintaining that they should be held liable for the learning and behavioral problems often suffered by lead-poisoned children. Lately, the food and beverage industry has started to feel the heat as well. Fearful of being held liable for the impacts of obesity on human health, McDonald's, Coca-Cola, and other companies have launched preemptive publicity campaigns urging consumers to straighten up and eat right.[86]

Nor does the game of "pin-the-responsibility-on-the-corporation" show any sign of stopping there. It has even been speculated that oil companies may eventually be held liable for the damage caused by climate change.[87]

The Senior Vice President then poses a question: Why are corporations generating so much hostility? Because they have the money and the power, she suggests, which always produces resentment along with admiration—but the reasons run deeper than that. And with that she turns the presentation over to the newly hired Vice President for Deep Strategy.

Things are going in the wrong direction, this gentleman says, and people know it. The environment is deteriorating and the social fabric is unraveling. Things seem increasingly out of control.

When things go wrong, people need someone to blame. Corporations make a ready target for this, and in fairness it must be said that to some degree they have earned it. The record is replete with examples of appalling corporate misdeeds, from raiding the till to jeopardizing workers to devastating entire ecosystems. Corporations have also been implicated in the breakdown of our democratic system, not through criminal activity but through the legally mandated right to support— okay, buy—political candidates. And this is something people understandably resent.

In addition, corporations are on the receiving end of enormous amounts of redirected rage. The tyranny of the objective is dragging the world into the abyss. At a level beneath conscious awareness, people sense this, if only because their inner lives are being disrupted, too. And so, along with all the other more straightforward reasons for being unhappy with corporations, people resent them because they are proxies for a domain that is widely if unconsciously viewed as responsible for much of what's wrong with the world.

A second intuition is operating here too, the Vice President for Deep Strategy continues. With the advent of globalization, the concept of the "global family" has made the transition from sentimental metaphor to something much closer to reality. And this global family is wildly dysfunctional. Without being able to articulate the situation in so many words, people know this to be the case, and they hold big business accountable.

How can a corporation even begin to respond to this unfortunate state of affairs? By addressing the dysfunctionality, that's how. By taking responsibility for the system in which it is complicit.

There are well-established rules for addressing dysfunctionality, he continues, and they apply regardless of the size or nature of the system.

First, since dysfunctionalities derive their strength from collectively held secrets, those secrets must be raised up and exposed to the light of day. Secrets lose their power to the extent that they are named.

Second, the beneficiaries of the dysfunctionality must disavow the system that's been supporting them and voluntarily commit to make things better. For example, if the dysfunctional system in question is a family protecting an alcoholic parent, he or she must admit to their dependency, else all is to no avail. He or she must rise to the intervention.

Corporations are the global equivalent of the alcoholic parent. It is they who for a century or more have buttressed and benefited from the tyranny of the objective—this is why they are so powerful and wealthy. They are the Big Daddy, or at least a Big Daddy, in our global dysfunctional family. Until they assume a leadership role in addressing the crisis in which they are so deeply implicated, the system is destined to remain at a standstill, spinning its wheels and grinding down the world.

It is too late for corporations to initiate the conversation, which has long since been launched by the antiglobalization movement. But there is nothing stopping them from assuming a leadership role in addressing the dysfunctionalities that are forging our contemporary wasteland.

How might this play out?, the Vice President for Deep Strategy asks, and promptly answers his own question. One possibility might be for Big Idea and other forward-thinking corporations to convene a Commission on Global Dysfunctionality with participation from all the major governance sectors, with a view toward collectively designing ways to effectively address the global sustainability crisis. One outcome of this process might be a commitment to mitigation strategies—every time a global company opens a store somewhere, it contributes to a fund supporting locally owned retail enterprises in that same area. Another might be corporate-sponsored educational programs warning people about the dangers of consumerism, much as food and beverage companies have started cautioning people about the dangers of unhealthy food.

Combine these with other forward-thinking strategies, and the result could be a nonviolent revolution, brought about by a collaborative process spearheaded by the readiness of a few bold corporations to work at a deep-structural level on behalf of the greater good.

One of Big Idea's most conventional thinkers raises his hand. "I don't get this at all," he says. "When you're in power, you have to hang onto that power! You can't relinquish it voluntarily! That's the way the game's been played for the last ten thousand years, and that's how it will be played for the next ten thousand years, too! Plus which, you have to remember that Big Idea is a corporation, not a do-good social organization. We have a legal duty to maximize return to investors. How is a strategy based on your "enlightened commitment" going to deliver that? What's the business case for this?"

"There's a considerable competitive advantage to be gained here," the Vice President for Deep Strategy replies. "In these anxiety-inducing times, people are desperate for leadership—and not what *passes* for leadership, not the leadership that recycles the truisms of the tyranny of the objective, but true leadership, leadership that is committed to righting imbalances and creating harmony at the deep-structural level. What a golden opportunity this leadership deficit offers to companies with the foresight and courage to seize the opportunity!

"Imagine how wide the differentiation will be," he continues, "between conventional companies and the handful of corporations that are prepared to step forward in this way. Conventional companies will continue to be widely perceived as the purveyors of a worldview that has been largely discredited by virtue of its association with the tyranny of the objective. Leadership companies will be viewed as rescuers, come from out of nowhere to save the day. If I were to ask you, "Would you rather have your customers view you as friend or foe?" the answer would be obvious, right? If, then, I were to ask you, "Would you rather have your customers view you as foe or hero?" the answer would be even more obvious, no? And how could stepping into the hero's role not create a sizable competitive advantage over conventional companies?

"Just as there is an upside to taking action, there is also a downside to not doing so," the Vice President for Deep Strategy continues. "Humanity will continue to drift toward the abyss, and corporations will risk a considerably more virulent backlash. When things go wrong, people seek out scapegoats. Sometimes it is the powerless that are on the receiving end of their rage, but just as often it is the powerful. Sacrificing the king is a primal cultural ritual, undertaken for millennia to preserve the cycle of the seasons and the social order. In our denatured world, there is no better 'king'—or target for scapegoating—than the multinational corporation."

The Vice President for Deep Strategy concludes with a brief story. "You all surely remember," he says, "the advertising campaign that launched our company on the road to success. 'What's the Big Idea?' the slogan went—and the 'Big Idea' was this company. You will also recall how that slogan was turned against us by antiglobalization activists, who had lumped us in with Starbucks and the rest. 'What's the Big Idea?' legions of their banners stated, spinning the slogan into a declaration of moral outrage. Now we come to a third type of 'Big Idea,' the possibility that this company could claim a position of 'deep leadership' in our global family, and gain a significant competitive advantage in the process."

ฅๆฅๆฅๆฅๆ

Will the Vice President of Deep Strategy prevail? Or will more cautious and conventional thinkers have their way? Unfortunately we will never know the answer to this question. Instead we must leave the assembled executives of Big Idea, Inc. behind—we can imagine them, if we like, poised in a state of suspended animation—and proceed on our way. Before doing so, though, we might note two things. First, deep strategy isn't only for corporations. Everyone has problems to solve; everyone has dysfunctionalities to contend with. The process and principles described above can be applied wherever there are imbalances and injustices to redress. Second, deep strategy is itself integral. In Big Idea's case, for instance, the proposed solutions are strategic—intended to create competitive advantage. They are socially responsible—they promote a step change increase in Big Idea's commitment to the society. And finally, they are sensitive to the meaning dimension—their greater goal is to promote harmony and happiness in the global human family. Deep strategy aligns global corporations with the greater good, an all-important transformation.

Engaging the Sage

The integral way is a higher-level way, a way that it becomes possible to practice only after having disidentified with the strategist, citizen, and seeker. The integral way is the way of the sage. But what does that mean, specifically? What differentiates the sage's way of doing things from that of other people? If we take a closer look at the habits of mind that characterize the sage, we find that there are five such habits, or practices, in all.

The Five Practices

Knowing the No and Yes of It. First, there is the habit of being constantly on the lookout for what we wish to shun, and the converse habit of remembering who we wish to be. The no and the yes of it: no to the dark enchantment in its many guises; yes to our own highest potential, steadfastly joyous, focused, and committed to playing our part in making things right in the world.

Practicing the "Three D's." Earlier in this chapter, we saw that the sage practices what we might call the "Three D's": deep awareness, deep responsibility, and deep strategy. *Deep awareness* entails understanding the work that needs to be done, both in oneself and in the world. *Deep responsibility* is the moral sense that translates that awareness into action. *Deep strategy* is the commitment to take action, optimized for success.

Befriending All Three Selves. The sage does not play favorites. The strategist, the citizen, and the seeker are all known, all appreciated, all respected. Their voices are all honored. The sage is a parent with three children, each of them equally loved.

Practicing Right Balance. A vast balancing act defines the sage's emotional and spiritual life. How many continuums there are in life to travel, and how many polarities to balance! The sage travels them all, and he or she does so without attachment, from the ideal to the real, from judgment to nonjudging, from despair to hope. Polarities that are honored include the masculine and the feminine, the comic sense and the tragic sense, the sacred and profane. There are selfishness and selflessness, thought and action, detachment and involvement, dominance and surrender. And behind all these and the many other polarities the sage travels, there towers the most powerful continuum (and greatest paradox) of all: the absolute preciousness of life, and the great indifferent wheel of life and death. Here, too, the sage resists attachment: he or she practices what Ken Wilber calls "passionate equanimity." And of course the respective interests of the citizen, the strategist, and the seeker must also be balanced. Right balance is the commitment to inclusiveness, engaged as an art form.

Honoring the Shadow. We all have preferences—vanilla ice cream over chocolate, stripes over solids, the depth dimension over the objective domain. The sage works constantly to override these biases, not when ordering ice cream, to be sure, but when the resulting behavior has significant practical consequences.

In Jungian terms, we all have a shadow, an aspect of ourselves that we are uncomfortable with and inclined to reject. This is a leading cause of realm wars. The sage understands this and makes a conscious practice of stepping toward his or her shadow. If I am distrustful of my depth-dimension self, I observe when I am triggered by it, and I do my best to develop a more compassionate attitude toward it. I seek, in other words, to better understand and ultimately to befriend that which I find threatening: I seek to encounter and, through kindness, slay the Minotaur within. Over time, this produces a double benefit: it makes for better dialogue and decision making by making us less reactive, and it makes us less afraid.

The Confessional Heart and the Lion Heart

When the term "culture wars" is used, it typically refers to the ideological battles between left and right, or between advocates of an open society and fundamentalists, and while these are indeed culture wars, there is yet another type of culture war that is frequently overlooked. This one pits action against reflection, citizens against seekers. It is a war without end, and a war in which neither side is completely in the right. Reflection without action can be as damaging as action without reflection; as our priests have been reminding us for years, there are sins of omission as well as sins of commission. For transformative results to be achieved, reflection must be married with action; the two must be integrated at a higher level. This is the work of the sage, whose special skill, in the end, is alchemy— the sage transmutes the lead of the three domains, all that "gross matter," into integral gold.

The cultural critic and Jungian psychologist James Hillman

puts an interesting twist on the culture war that pits the seeker against the citizen when he contrasts the "confessional heart," which he derives from Augustine, with the *"coeur de lion,"* or lion heart. The former is inner-directed and revelatory; the latter takes its passions directly out into the world. The heart of Augustine, according to Hillman, is largely self-absorbed, committed to working through its intrapsychic issues alone, or through "secular sharing in group confession," which I understand to mean twelve-step programs, men's groups, and the like. The result: "subjectivisms without rage," a commitment to relativism that makes us all solely responsible for our "stuff" and strips the anger out of everything.[88]

By contrast, Hillman writes, "Crucial to the heart of the lion is that it believes, and it believes that it does not think. So its thought appears in the world as project, desire, concern, mission. Thinking and doing together. This is the bold thought that takes us into battle, for Mars rides a red lion, and the heroes—David, Samson, Hercules—must meet the ravenous hunger for the world of deeds fulminating in their expansive chests."[89]

So which is it to be? The self-doubting, sensitive heart of Augustine, or the self-confident warrior's unthinking plunge into action? Hillman is plainly fed up with the confessional mode and wants to see more people dive into direct engagement with the world. If their fuel happens to be anger, that's okay. The confessional mode is debilitating because it turns anger into a character weakness, or psychological "stuff," that needs to be "worked through." For Hillman, the confessional world-view transforms an entirely legitimate sense of outrage into an emotional liability that people try to deal with through depth-dimension, inner work. When this happens, something else happens, too: civic action born in outrage is paralyzed—what is actually justifiable action is twisted into mere "acting out." In this way, the confessional heart removes us from civic life and plunges us into narcissistic self-absorption. Hillman's views are, in this particular respect, surprisingly similar to those of

conservatives like Christopher Lasch and Robert Bork, who, as
we saw in Chapter 6, share Hillman's disdain for depth-dimension self-absorption.

For Hillman, too much looking inward is a form of denial,
as harmful in its way as the massive, systematic denial that
fuels the tyranny of the objective. *We've Had a Hundred Years of
Psychotherapy and the World's Getting Worse*, he laments in the
book of the same name, coauthored with Michael Ventura.
Rage is a healthy response to the depredations being perpetrated
on the planet.

But action—the lion heart—is dangerous, and in more ways
than one. People who take their hearts out into the world put
their lives at risk, and not just theoretically. Real action makes
real enemies, as proven by the fate of lion hearts like Mohandas
Gandhi and Martin Luther King. The confessional heart, by
contrast, offers a sort of refuge for the insecure. To the best of
my knowledge, no one has ever gotten murdered in a men's
group. Insecure? Fearful? Turn inward, where the worst you'll
face is the idea, not the reality, of death!

The impetuous lion heart is dangerous in another way too.
It can take us into wrong-headed, destructive action. One of the
catchphrases in the sustainability community is "unintended
consequences"—actions that produce unforeseen effects. Chlo-
rofluorocarbons that destroy the ozone layer, carbon dioxide
emissions that raise the atmospheric temperature, and chemicals that disrupt endocrine function are all examples of unintended consequences. The lion heart leaps before it looks, and
the result is often unintended consequences.

Indeed, the twentieth century can be seen as the century of
lion-hearted action, in which people acted on their beliefs, their
passions, their insights, with often horrific consequences. Lion-
hearted engagement has given us serial genocide (was ever a
man more lion-hearted than Hitler?) and is now hurtling us
toward an ecological catastrophe of unprecedented proportions.
In 1921, William Butler Yeats wrote the prescient and now-

famous phrase in his poem "The Second Coming": "*The best lack all conviction, while the worst/Are full of passionate intensity.*" This can be read as an indictment of the lion-hearted impulse, and as praise for the confessional heart.

It is now eighty years later and many of "the best" are still traumatized, more so now than ever. The century's depredations ripped the lion heart out of the chests of many people and sent them into support groups for confessional sharings. The times, however, call for heroic engagement, and that cannot be entered into from the fallout shelters of our in-turned selves. We must reclaim our lion's heart, but not in a way that recapitulates the horrors of the past century. How do we claim the boldness to act and the humility to remain attentive to the limits of our knowledge? How do we integrate doubt and certainty, inquiry and action? How do we plunge into self, and plunge into society, and take the best of each and leave the worst behind? How do we integrate the confessional heart and the lion's heart, introversion and extroversion, the depth dimension and society? This is the work of the sage, and crucially important work it is, too, for what our times require is not merely the familiar citizenship of yesterday's civics classes, but a postconventional "new citizenship" that integrates action and reflection into a form of engagement whose goal is right balance in the world.

Yeats's "The Second Coming" closes with: "*And what rough beast, its hour come round at last/Slouches towards Bethlehem to be born?*" I like to think that some new beast, brave but not rough, is being forged in the gentle fires of depth-dimension confessionals around the country and the world. I like to imagine that a very private alchemical marriage is taking place between the confessional heart and the lion heart—between the seeker and the citizen—and that the integral beast that emerges will come out striding, not slouching, and committed to redeeming the world.

CHAPTER 11
OUT OF THE LABYRINTH

At Home in the Garden of Words

For fifteen years or so, from the time I went away to college in 1966 to my parents' death in 1979, I was mired in a realm war with my father. It wasn't a shooting war. I don't recall us ever shouting at each other. It was more a Cold War, or rather a Cool War. Pursed lips where there might have been laughter, and that grating sense of not being heard.

Most of all, there was the feeling of being trapped in a cul-de-sac. The tension between us was part of the order of things, as unalterable in its way as my having an older sister or a male body. It never occurred to me to try to resolve things with my father. He was the knowledgeable one, after all, not I. Initiating a conversation with him would have felt preposterously presumptuous, like throwing down a challenge to God. I might as well have aspired to change the color of the sky.

I suspect my father felt equally frustrated. He loved me, of that I have no doubt, but I was a puzzle to him. How could I be so uncertain of my direction, or so susceptible to the blandishments of my time? For my father, the contours of the struggle were clear, and it troubled him that his son, his blood and sole male heir, was not on the battlements alongside him.

More than once, he spoke to me in cautionary tones of people he called "trimmers," figures in Dante's *Divine Comedy* who were condemned to a sort of anteroom of hell. Trimmers never took sides but followed a forever-shifting banner. In Dante's words, they "lived without infamy and without praise... [They] were not rebels, nor were faithful to God, but were for themselves. The heavens chased them out in order to not be less beautiful, nor does the deep Hell receive them, for the damned would have some boast of them.... These wretches...were never alive." And this, my father seemed to be saying, would be my destiny, if only metaphorically, if I did not figure out who I was and take a stand for what I believed in. I needed to be like him, in other words.

My main confusion, I now understand, was around the depth dimension. It attracted me, it threatened me, it rattled and agitated me. I didn't know what to make of it, or (to paraphrase Gertrude Stein) if there even *was* a "there there," if it really existed at all.

My father had none of this ambivalence. For him the depth dimension was something to be shunned, the repository of all that was unfocused and unformed.

I can empathize with this; I do have my father's genes, after all. My father loved clarity and precision. In addition to being a man of letters, he was also a man of words—and words, and sentences, and paragraphs, when strung together in nice neat logical rows, create a pleasing sense of order and coherence. He was a gardener of ideas, and his tool was language, and he navigated this manicured land with deftness and delight. But something precedes language: the thing the word describes, the experience itself. "We have more than we can know. We know more than we can say," Wendell Berry writes, and this other world, this depth-dimension world beyond the reach of words, discomfited my father and made him scowl.[90] It wasn't elegant, as the garden was. It wasn't namable or knowable. It was sloppy and unformed and off-putting.

From one perspective, this antipathy was inexplicable. My father was a humanist, after all, and humanists study the humanities, which my dictionary defines as "the branches of learning concerned with human thought and relations, as distinguished from the sciences; especially, literature and philosophy, and often, the fine arts, history, etc." This sounds suspiciously like the material of the depth dimension, yet this was precisely the domain my father turned away from.

The explanation for this apparent contradiction lies in the

fact that my father was a *secular* humanist, a *rational* humanist—which is to say, a humanist of the objective domain. For him, the depth dimension smacked of religiosity, and religiosity meant Christianity, and Christianity, as it had played out over the past two millennia, meant power disguised as principle, guilt imposed on the susceptible, irrationality run amok, and the suppression of free inquiry. It meant hypocrisy and self-righteousness, dogmatism and superstition. It meant monks flogging themselves and soldiers wearing crosses and the *auto-da-fés* of the Inquisition. This was the world my father saw when he peered into the depth dimension.

This distaste in turn extended to the depth dimension in all its masks and forms. It was the irrational that my father most of all deplored, as exemplified, for instance, by religious superstition, but he extended this antipathy to those aspects of experience that aren't irrational so much as non-rational, even though there is a very considerable difference between the two. Irrationality is the opposite of rationality: it means unreasonable, unfounded, ill-conceived. Irrationality is reason, practiced badly. A trance brought about by ecstatic dancing or drumming is certainly not rational, but it isn't irrational, either. It's non-rational—it belongs to another category of experience entirely. Indeed, much of its value lies quite precisely in the fact that it takes us on a holiday away from reason—it takes us out of our heads, as they say. This distinction escaped my father, though. The material of the depth dimension was all of a piece to him, all unprovable and preverbal and worthy only of impatience.

To take one of many possible examples, "being" is a depth-dimension concept that annoyed him no end. Erich Fromm writes:

> [T]he *Great Masters of Living* have made the alternative between having and being a central issue of their respective systems. The Buddha teaches that in order to arrive at the highest stage of human development, we must not crave possessions. Jesus teaches: "For whosoever will save his life

shall lose it; but whosoever will lose his life for my sake, the same shall save it. For what is a man advantaged, if he gain the whole world, and lose himself, or be cast away?" (Luke 9:24-25). Master Eckhart taught that to have nothing and to make oneself open and "empty," not to let one's ego stand in one's way, is the condition for achieving spiritual wealth and strength. Marx taught that luxury is as much a vice as poverty and that our goal should be to be much, not to have much.[91]

Having inhabits the objective domain and society, while *being* is depth-dimensional. One *has* ideas, one *has* strategies—these forms of possession reside in the objective domain. One also *has* a public self that one takes out into the field of action, out into society. By contrast, one simply *"is"* in the depth dimension.

My father just didn't get it. In 1959 he recorded a series of dialogues with John Fischer of *Harper's* magazine. On one of the recordings, he says:

> *Or [consider] non-being. There's a good deal of this [the use of language with no clear meaning], which frankly raises my hackles, in contemporary existentialism. An awful lot of this, when you talk about the "courage to be." Now, I can give some meaning to the phrase, "the courage to be a martyr," "the courage to be a businessman," "the courage to be a fool," "the courage to be a philosopher," if you want, "the courage to be a man." But when you cut it off and say, "the courage to be," I'm afraid it leaves me completely not so much unmoved as inert. I have no idea what is being said, and I have no idea how any of the statements made by people who talk this way could possibly be refuted.*[92]

This is a gracious formulation, the public formulation of a tactful man, but the underlying message is clear. "'*Being*'?" my father was saying. "What sort of nonsense is '*being*'?"

In another dialogue, my father waxes skeptical about

ecstatic indigenous celebrations:

> Frankel: [*Philosophy's*] *ultimate function, I think, is that it contributes to people's self-consciousness, to their awareness. It heightens consciousness.... [I]t seems to me that we people here on this planet just have one time around, as it were, and it's a shame to waste this time around by not being clear about what we think and why we think so. I think that if we are not conscious of what we think and why we think so, how we behave, why we behave so, whether we believe that we are following a rational principle in behaving in some way or a conventional principle, we're wasting our most fundamental opportunity, which is to be intensely alive.*

> Fischer: *And as you suggested earlier, this is the distinguishing mark between a civilized and uncivilized man.*

> Frankel: *This gives you another way of judging the value of a civilization. A great many people, I think, react against the strain of civilization because it is a strain. It goes with self-doubt, with inquiry, with a certain degree of uncertainty. Its great reward is intensity of experience. I think the difference between a civilized life and an uncivilized life is essentially a difference between intensity of experience and monotony. I think we often think of savage life as terribly intense and unrepressed, but I think that the kind of hysterical frenzies you sometimes see in primitive societies—wild dances and all the rest—are the occasional outbursts of people who most of the time are living on the level of sheer routine and habit. Now, philosophy's great function is to shake up your habits, shake up your routines, and make you notice what's going on.*

> Fischer: *This is what Socrates meant when he said that "the unexamined life is not worth living."*

> Frankel: *Yes.*[93]

This amounts to a paean to cognition, and a perfectly

understandable one it is. Certainly philosophical self-scrutiny
has much to recommend it. But in fairness, if one is going to
engage in self-scrutiny, shouldn't every aspect of one's being be
put under the microscope? My father's attempt to explain
ecstatic depth-dimension rites was strictly sociological: he made
no attempt to understand the experience subjectively. For him
it was axiomatic that the life of a "civilized" person, which is to
say the life of a person living in the objective domain, is more
intense than the less self-reflective existence of an indigenous
tribesperson. The urbane and cosmopolitan approach to life was
richer, fuller and in the end more meaningful than a life inter-
spersed with ecstatic encounters with the gods. Of this he was
certain, even though he had never, so far as I know, experienced
the alternative. This seems rather unfair of him and maybe
even priggish, like saying one doesn't like dancing, or sex, or
LSD, without ever trying them.

This didn't stop my father, though. From his perch in the
objective domain, there in his enchanting word-garden, he
knew what he knew. He knew it *a priori*, which is to say, he
knew it in precisely the same way the true believer "knows" a
truth revealed by God. My father's faith, though, was the faith
of reason, and on this he was non-negotiable. Up with the objective domain, down with the depth dimension!

I Wonder Where the Wonder Went

And so I wonder how he would have felt had he been sitting
next to my wife Deborah and me one sunny day in May 2000 on
a bench in the San Francisco Aquarium. We were in a long corridor: sharks and other great ocean fish were patrolling the tank
behind our heads. I just had come from the aquarium's collec-
tion of seahorses. Such extraordinary creatures, these exquisite
miniatures, entwining around each other like the most tender of
lovers! Seeing them had sent me into something like an altered
state. I was feeling enraptured.

What I had just been vouchsafed, I realized, was wonder—
wonder at what I will call God's grandeur. The seahorses had

granted me a gift, the gift of the depth dimension. Seeing them had cracked open the shell of my strategist self and exposed me to the miracle and majesty of nature.

I then shared with Deborah a thought that seemed transparently obvious to me in the clear light of that moment. Our great challenge, I said, was to get out from under the tyranny of the objective, and wonder did that. Wonder opened the heart. It inspired humility and caring and compassion. It returned us to our place in the depth dimension, to our home inside the great web. Wonder could become a strategy, a way to consciously engage the energies of the depth dimension.

If my father had been there, I daresay he would have rolled his eyes at this, but it was Deborah who was sitting beside me, not my father, and she nodded in agreement. If there was such a thing as a politics of meaning, she wondered aloud, why not a politics of wonder?

My encounter with the seahorses was not wholly positive, though. Their beauty was too much for me. My soul opened briefly to the rapture, then went into headlong retreat. A part of me wanted no part of wonder. By the time Deborah and I had stood up to move on from the corridor, I could feel my defenses shooting up around me like shields in a science-fiction movie.

I spent much of the rest of the day musing about this. Why, I asked myself, this resistance? What compelled me to erect this barrier between myself and wonder?

At one level, I soon realized, my reaction had been entirely predictable. God's grandeur always terrifies us mortals. From the poet Rainer Maria Rilke's first *Duino Elegy*:

> *Who, if I cried, would hear me among the angelic orders?*
> *And even if one of them suddenly /pressed me against his*
> *heart, I should fade in the strength of his stronger existence.*
> *For Beauty's nothing/ but the beginning of Terror we're still*
> *just able to bear, and why we adore it so is because it*
> *serenely/ disdains to destroy us. Every single angel is terrible.*

On further reflection, however, I decided there might also

be an explanation that was unique to my generation. It is always the lot of children to absorb the hidden currents of their environment and time, and beneath the creature comforts of our lives, we baby boomers had some heavy traumas to absorb. I emerged into the world in 1950, a scant five years after the Holocaust and the Bomb had exploded into our consciousness, etching a new and nightmarish vision of the human condition into our souls. The Cold War with its MAD promise of Mutually Assured Destruction was just taking hold. In one of my earliest childhood recollections, I am walking with my classmate Paul Galdone to the school bus. The year, if memory serves, is 1956. To our left there is a narrow row of pine trees and, behind it, farmer George Smith's pumpkin patch. I am telling Paul with some satisfaction that at least we have the Bomb and the Russians don't. No, he corrects me, the Russians have it too. To this day, I recall how my heart tightened as this terrible knowledge took hold.

Even if the specific circumstances of our childhoods were sunny, and mine were, the backdrop against which they unfolded was nightmarish. We baby boomers were the children of the Bomb, the children of the Holocaust. This is the stuff our dreams were made of. Was this why I shut down—and why, if I am not mistaken, many of my peers shut down too? It seems a reasonable supposition: how can one be expected to sustain one's sense of wonder when the imagination, if granted permission to open, delivers one into a landscape whose contours are fearsome beyond imagining?

So there we young Boomers were, with a pair of great horrors to avoid, and to make matters worse, during the fifties, television came along. It was the tyranny of the objective's most powerful weapon yet in its arsenal of distractions. The screen rapidly became, well, my *screen*—my protective barrier, my consolation. By the time my parents came home with their first TV in 1956, I was already a junkie-in-waiting, and I became a junkie-in-practice in no time flat. Nothing thrilled me more than watching TV. I lived for *Zorro* and *Dobie Gillis*. The pixels' flickering glimmer became my warm blue womb.

Here, too, I was one among many. Television was the anti-dote to horror for an entire generation. And so we stared, and grew flat and dumb. By the time television had had its way with us, our capacity for wonder had shrunk to almost nothing.

By the Time We Got to Woodstock

And then, deep into the 1960s, along came Woodstock. Vietnam, Timothy Leary, marijuana, LSD: all this cracked the egg and plunged us into a wildly upside-down world. The depth dimension asserted itself floridly.

Timothy Leary anticipated mass enlightenment; mass chaos happened instead. It was all too much, too soon—anarchistic, not integrative—and it produced what in retrospect emerges as a sort of national psychosis. The forces of the depth dimension clashed head-on with the defenders of the tyranny of the objective, and the resulting conflict split the cultural fabric into two. The center could not hold; a schizoid break resulted.

In due course the forces of tradition and authority reasserted themselves (remember the "Moral Majority?"), the culture got "sane" again (or if not sane, "normal"), and all the house revisionists started cranking out the Official Story. It had been temporary insanity, it had been a reaction to Vietnam, it had been an overdose of licentiousness, but that was then and this was now and things were back on course, thank goodness. And indeed it had been all of that, but far more fundamentally it had been a cosmic energetic uprising, based on a deeply intuitive and profoundly accurate sense of what was wrong with the world.

As for me, I graduated from college in 1970. Final exams were cancelled during my senior year to protest the American invasion of Cambodia. The decision to do this was reached at a massive gathering of students and faculty in the university's spanking new gymnasium. I believe the vote was 4,000-plus in favor of striking, and twelve against.

My first encounter with drugs came on the last day of my

freshman year in 1967, at a party celebrating the end of exams. A distant acquaintance whispered conspiratorially to a companion, "Hey, let's go roll us some Zig-zags." I had no idea what a Zig-zag was until a friend enlightened me. It seemed they were a brand of rolling paper and this had been a discussion about marijuana. This revelation made me feel appalled, intrigued, and quite adventuresome and grown-up.

Then the storm broke. A year later, Zig-zags and the other accoutrements of pot culture were everywhere. The politics got heavy. A roommate joined the radical Students for a Democratic Society (SDS) and railed at us regularly about the military-industrial complex. Late in my senior year, a student I had known since high school was arrested for trying to burn down a campus building.

A strange new world had opened up, and I was a babe wandering through it. I attended a few SDS meetings but never joined. I was one among the hundreds of thousands in the massive March on Washington protesting the war in Vietnam, but I thought of myself as more observer than participant. I tried mescaline, played in an intramural hockey game and was promptly penalized two minutes for tripping. I did my rather feeble best to reap the fruits of free love.

As confused and overstimulated as I was, my father was dismayed. In 1965 he had accepted a State Department appointment as Assistant Secretary of State for Educational and Cultural Affairs. Two years later he resigned, not so much in protest over Vietnam, although he did oppose the war, as in frustration over the fact that the war was draining funding from his programs. Back at Columbia, he watched the goings-on with consternation. Students took over a building and defecated on a teacher's desk. Another professor's research papers, the product of years of work, were destroyed. Vulgar, cruel acts like this my father deplored. More broadly, he was horrified by the protestors' readiness to ride roughshod over democratic processes. Yet he was not entirely unsympathetic. He thought the war in Vietnam was a terrible mistake, and he believed students should be cut some slack in their learning years. In 1972 he published a novel called *A Stubborn Case*. It told the story of John Burgess, a world-weary professor who watches the campus events of the late-sixties unfold through sometimes tipsy eyes. It is all a little crazy; irrationality abounds on both sides. Burgess becomes friendly with a student named Otto who in the book's climax dies when he is caught between the demonstrators and the authorities.

My father portrayed Otto as a well-intentioned, somewhat confused person who while sympathetic to the radicals was not one of them, and was simply trying to make sense of it all. For all I know, I was the model for Otto.

In our personal life, as opposed to his fiction, my father was less sympathetic. My affectations and affections grated on him. During spring break of my sophomore year, I visited my parents in Aspen, where Dad was teaching a seminar at the Aspen Institute for Humanistic Studies. In the flamboyant spirit of the times, I was sporting what a ski instructor called a "Zorro hat." I suspect my father thought I looked foolish, and he was probably right.

And then there was my infatuation with dubious characters like the Zen Buddhist Alan Watts. For my father, the esteem in which many members of my generation held Watts was entirely unwarranted. Watts claimed to be a philosopher but in my father's eyes he was much less than that, a fuzzy-brained preacher-man, a man incapable of critical thinking, one of those clueless souls who prated endlessly about things like pure being. In Dad's view, Watts was a pied piper, leading a generation to drowning. I remember one time during those years when I had the temerity to bring up Watts's name at dinner. My father's annoyance was palpable. I could almost feel the silver shake.

Another writer who got my father's goat was Aldous Huxley. Not the early or middle Huxley, during which time he penned such memorable works as *Point Counter Point* and *Brave New World*: the Huxley of his later years. When Huxley was in his late fifties, he tried mescaline and this opened the depth dimension to him. This long-time and celebrated citizen of the objective domain promptly became an advocate of psychedelic consciousness. The title of his short book, *The Doors of Perception*, which was published in 1954, came from a poem by Blake: *"If the doors of perception were cleansed every thing would appear to man as it is, infinite."* The rock group The Doors took their name from the same line.

Huxley's transformation into high-brow drug advocate earned him hero status in the emerging hippie culture of the sixties. I read *The Doors of Perception* in 1970, and it blew my mind. Among his peers, including my father, it dropped him off the charts. For them, this was professional senility.

Beyond the Shallows of Right and Wrong

Back home from San Francisco and the aquarium, I picked up a copy of Huxley's utopian and transparently post-mescaline novel *Island*. It isn't a great work of fiction—it's a novel of ideas, and that may be an oxymoron—but it presents a provocative vision of the ideal world. It tells the story of Will Farnaby, a jaded journalist who finds himself on Pala, an island state where wisdom and higher consciousness are the rule. All the citizens of the island take a hallucinogen, a *"moksha*-medicine" (*moksha* is the Sanskrit term for enlightenment), that plugs them into the cosmic verities. This knowledge makes them wise, and because they are wise they create wise institutions and live in harmony.

I was just finishing the book when I was graced by a powerful synchronicity, Carl Jung's term for a meaningful coincidence. On the morning of the day in question, I happened on a passage in the series of recordings my father made with John Fischer during which he speaks sympathetically about logical positivism, a philosophical school that is very pro-science and impatient, to put it mildly, with abstract metaphysics. The *Encyclopedia Brittanica* defines logical positivism as "a philosophical doctrine formulated in Vienna in the 1920s, according to which scientific knowledge is the only kind of factual knowledge and all traditional metaphysical doctrines are to be rejected as meaningless."[94] Whatever else we might say about logical positivism, it is plainly a philosophy of the objective domain.

Coincidentally, a few hours later I finished reading *Island*. In the climactic scene, the journalist Will Farnaby takes the vaunted *moksha*-medicine (psilocybin? mescaline?). It is a transformative experience. Deep into his trip, he puts Bach's Fourth Brandenburg Concerto onto the stereo and is dazzled by what he hears. There are three instruments, the violin, the recorder, and the harpsichord, each of which makes its own unique contribution. The recorders bespeak "pure contemplation, unconcerned, beyond contingency, outside the context of moral judgments." There is the violin, accompanying the recorders' "contemplative detachment" with the "notes of passionate involvement." And surrounding them both are the "sharp, dry notes" of the harpsichord. "Spirit and instinct, action and vision—and around them the web of intellect," Huxley writes.[95]

Reading these words, I harked to full attention. Huxley was describing the triad.

The "*contemplative detachment*," "*spirit*," and "*vision*" of the recorders—these were terms for the depth dimension.

The violin's "*instinct*," "*action*," and "*passionate involvement*" described society.

And the harpsichord's tones, which produced the "*web of intellect*"—this was the voice of the objective domain.

Then came the synchronistic clincher:

> "*It's like a Logical Positivist*," Farnaby said.
> "*What is?*"
> "*The harpsichord.*"
> *Like a Logical Positivist, he was thinking in the shallows of his mind, while in the depths the great Event of light and sound timelessly unfolded....*[96]

This was the same logical positivism about which, a few hours earlier, I had heard my father speak so favorably. Huxley's characterization threw me for a loop. Was this really what my father was, my good and wise and noble father, a man "thinking in the shallows of his mind?"

It was a memorably unpleasant moment. It wasn't that Huxley's words condemned my father so much as that they had caused me to do so. I loved and admired my father, that much I knew. I adored him, even. I was immensely proud of him for being so revered. Yet I was also furious with him. I felt forsaken and betrayed because what I in many ways experienced as my truest essence, my depth-dimension self, had over and over again been denied and consigned to the shadows by him. Where was the truth in this, or wisdom? Yes, I loved him, but there now arose in me the conviction that I was wrong to love a man who could deny me in this way. My love for him was misbegotten, which meant that the world that admired him so much must be misbegotten, too. And so I was torn in two. I wanted to defend the man I admired and adored, and I was also filled with forgotten rage. Yes, that *was* my father, a man thinking in the shallows of his mind, a man who would not open eyes and heart and clearly see his own son!

There was something else as well. I was and am my father's son; I carry his genes inside me. His handwriting and mine, once very different, are now almost identical. I have a way of pensively placing my lower lip over my upper one that I got from him, not from observing him but, I am convinced, through genetic inheritance. If my father was a man thinking in the shallows of his mind, then I almost surely was, too.

These painful feelings badly wanted resolution, and fortunately this happened soon. The next day, Deborah directed me to another passage in the recordings:

Fischer: *How did it happen that you got interested in it [philosophy]?*

Frankel: *Perhaps the person who made the choice is the last person to give the right answer, but as I look back on my education in high school and in college, I remember that I was terribly interested in the relations between different fields of experience. I was fascinated by science and enchanted by what I saw in certain religions. I was also troubled by certain things about science and by things I saw in religion. I remember having a very great interest in poetry, but wondering what it was that the poets did to the practical world. And again, I recall having a considerable interest in politics and social affairs, and wondering what relationship the practical politician or the social reformer had to the man of ideas. What do politics and ideas have to say to each other, as it were? I think this was one of the things that first got me started, just my sense that human beings are engaged in a wide variety of quite different activities, that they use words and language and ideas in all these activities, but the activities don't seem to fit together and neither do the ideas and the language that they use seem to fit together, and I wondered how to do it. So I guess I was off in philosophy.* [97]

As I listened to these words, I could feel my heart opening to my father. How little I had known him! I had not known, for instance, that he had been drawn to philosophy by the sense that he inhabited dramatically different worlds, that they were all fascinating, and that they connected in mysterious ways. For him, philosophy had been a love affair with these worlds and their mysteries:

[T]his was one of the things that first got me started, just my sense that human beings are engaged in a wide variety of quite different activities, that they use words and language and ideas in all these activities, but the activities don't seem to fit together and neither do the ideas and the language that they use seem to fit together, and I wondered how to do it.

My father's love affair with philosophy had lasted all his life. He pursued it responsibly and passionately—he was the best sort of lover—and it made him a citizen of the objective domain. These words could have been my words. Like me, my father had been seeking an integral vision.

My journey has taken me elsewhere, but who am I to make my father wrong? Right and wrong are shallow thoughts. Like me, my father loved the three domains. Like me, he loved how they dance together. In a recent dream, I saw my father looking through a window at me from another dimension. He tossed me something, special information that floated to me on wings made of something like origami, and as I reached up to catch it I knew not to be afraid. The window wasn't really there; he and I had never really been apart. Father and son, life and death: these were shallow words. Words without meaning.

Following the Thread

In the 1970s, my father took up golf and sometimes we played together, striking terror in the hearts of foursomes on neighboring fairways. On one of those outings together, he told me I was his best friend. I was caught off guard completely. I was deeply aware of the silences between us and didn't know what to say. I remember the thoughts that ran through my mind. He was a vital man surrounded by people who loved him. Was our congenial but cautious relationship really the best, in terms of intimacy, he could do? What did he talk about with the people I thought of as his close friends? Was he simply being kind to me?

Now, going on thirty years later, another possibility occurs to me. Perhaps he could sense the bond that I was still too young to appreciate. And I *was* young—unformed too, even at his death in 1979, when I was twenty-nine and, more than many of my peers, still confused and searching. The Scottish poet Edwin Muir writes, in his great poem "The Labyrinth":

> Since I emerged that day from the labyrinth,
> Dazed with the tall and echoing passages,
> The swift recoils, so many I almost feared
> I'd meet myself returning at some smooth corner,
> Myself or my ghost, for all there was unreal

> *After the straw ceased rustling and the bull*
> *Lay dead upon the straw and I remained,*
> *Blood-splashed, if dead or alive I could not tell*
> *In the twilight nothingness (I might have been*
> *A spirit seeking his body through the roads*
> *Of intricate Hades)....*

When my father died, I was still in that labyrinth. That is not the case any longer; at least, I no longer feel that way. Sometimes I survey the time that has passed since then, and think of how I have changed, and I wonder what I would say to him. I would want to give him a sense of who I have become, and why, and the ways in which time has proven him and me to be alike, despite my ardent efforts when I was young to be so very different. And at the center of the conversation would be the integral way. I would try to explain to him why it has become an organizing principle, a way of life, for me.

To do so I would have to explain how these past mad decades have felt to me, this cocoon of time and circumstance I have been trying my best to burst free from all these years. I would try to convey to him what it felt like to come of age in that crazy, mixed-up world, dazed by the sixties, dazzled by the glitz and flash that followed. So much spectacle, so much energy, so much entropy...everything coming apart even as it sparkled and glowed. It was like living inside a grand fireworks display, simultaneously exciting and enervating—and yes, those were our souls drifting down depleted from the sky.

My father had grown up in a time that, while haunted by the specter of evil, was essentially intact and coherent. Not I, and not my generation. By the time we came of age, modernism was being blown into smithereens and what was being dynamited, among other things, was our sense of self. Where, how, could we find our center amidst all this chaos? This was the question I struggled with, without even knowing I was struggling with it, for years.

At an abstract level my father understood this, but not from the inside. He looked at me and saw what he was not, a soul without a center, and could not bring himself to smile. And then he died, and another decade passed, and then the integral way came along, and it brought me my "enlightenment."

A quarter-century has passed since my father died. That is a lot of time, and no time at all. If he were to visit me today, I would tell him about my journey and I would tell him about the integral way. I would also tell him about the sustainability crisis that has us careering like drunks on a bender toward a dark and dismal future. And finally, I would tell him why the integral way, coupled with sustainable development, has become a faith for me, as reason, that product of an earlier Enlightenment, was a faith for him.

When modernism died, we were plunged into a labyrinth. We had no maps, no real understanding of where we were, or who, or our direction. The triad and integral way provide a map that can help us find our way out. And not just any way out, but a path that is moral—virtuous, in the truest sense of the term; and right-thinking; and emotionally bracing; and heroic, even; and, when you think about it, really the only choice we have, given the task at hand.

Time is growing short. We must find our way out of the labyrinth. I say this to the spirit of my father, and I also say it to the spirits on the other side of these pages whose choices, today and tomorrow, will shape the future for untold generations to come. We have been given a gift, a thread, to guide us out of the labyrinth. It is here. It awaits us, this thread glittering like gold. We need only take it up and follow it.

A Glossary

The Triad
A framework for understanding ourselves and our created world. It proposes that there co-exist inside our psyches three fundamentally different ways of being in the world, and that we project these reality tunnels onto our institutions and culture. These three 'reality tunnels' are the objective domain, the social domain, and the depth dimension, respectively. If we think of them as subpersonalities, they are the strategist (the objective domain), the citizen (the social domain), and the seeker (the depth dimension).

The Objective Domain
This way of being in the world is 'objective' in two senses: it is focused on objectives, that is, end goals, and it favors objectivity (as distinguished from subjectivity). Its style is strategic, rational, analytical and linear.

The Strategist
The name ascribed to the subpersonality who inhabits the objective domain.

The Social Domain
This reality tunnel centers on our relationship with what psychologists call the 'other', a category that includes other people, the artifacts people create, and the natural world. It is a tribal and Darwinian space, and it also a space that carries with it both rights and responsibilities.

The Citizen
The subpersonality who inhabits the social domain.

The Depth Dimension
Where we go to discover meaning. It can be understood in many different ways: as the personal or collective unconscious, as the mythic imagination, as the seat of our spirituality, as the id, and more. It is also the darkness where we hide our secrets.

The Seeker
The aspect of ourselves that is engaged in the search for meaning.

The Tyranny of the Objective
A pattern in which the objective reality tunnel becomes the psychological or cultural norm, and the depth dimension is devalued.

A GLOSSARY

The Dark Enchantment
The spell cast over individuals as a result of long-term exposure to the tyranny of the objective.

Realm Wars
Competition among the strategist, citizen and seeker.

The Henry Higgins Fallacy
The utopian longing to inhabit a world where everyone share's one's own reality tunnel.

The Integral Way
The art of balancing the needs and values of the strategist, the citizen and the seeker in a manner that serves harmony and justice, at the personal, interpersonal, institutional or broader cultural level.

The Sage
The subpersonality, latent but 'actualizable' in all of us, who practices the integral way.

Deep Strategy
An approach to problem-solving that is based on the 'deep structural' dynamics underlying personal, interpersonal, institutional and cultural dysfunctionality.

The 'Three D's'
The 'Three D's' stands for 'deep responsibility,' 'deep awareness,' and 'deep strategy.' They describe the sage's mode of participation in the social, depth and strategic domains, respectively.

Right Balance
The term of art for the practice of heeding and balancing the needs of the strategist, citizen and seeker—and, more broadly, for honoring the many polarities and continuums in life.

The New Citizenship
An approach to civic commitment that emerges from the individual's sense of authenticity and personal responsibility, as distinguished from his or her sense of duty.

ENDNOTES

1 From Edwin Muir, The Brothers, *The Norton Anthology of Poetry* (New York: W.W. Norton, 1983), pp. 993-994.

2 Paul Hawken, Possibilities, in *Imagine: What America Could Be in the 21st Century*, edited by Marianne Williamson (Emmaus, PA: Rodale Press, 2000), p. 3.

3 In this book, I have little to say about my mother, Helen Frankel. This is because this particular story happens to be about my father and me, not my mother and me. She occupied – and still occupies – as large a place in my heart.

4 http://www.onelook.com/?w=worldview&ls=a

5 James Burke and Robert Ornstein, *The Axemaker's Gift: A Double-Edged History of Human Culture* (New York: Grosset/Putnam, 1995), p. xvi.

6 A third view holds that once you strip away mental operations and social customs, you are left with nothing at all. There are only our 'socially constructed' realities and no such thing as the depth dimension. This view came into vogue in the 20th Century and remains with us today. While it claims to cut through superstition and reveal the way things really are, it can also be seen as a form of servitude to the tyranny of the objective.

7 Quoted in Robert Coles, *The Secular Mind* (Princeton, NJ: Princeton University Press, 1999), pp. 143-144

8 See http://www.princeton.edu/~pear/2.html.

9 Vladimir Nabokov, *Ada* (New York: McGraw-Hill, 1969), p. 174.

10 This is precisely the same strategy organizations like Amnesty International and Transparency International use. They heal social and political wounds by dragging torture and corruption into the light.

11 Examples include *You Don't Understand Me*, by Deborah Tannen, *In a Different Voice: Psychological Theory and Women's Development*, by Carol Gilligan, and *Men Are From Mars, Women Are From Venus*, by John Gray.

12 Jesse H. Wright, M.D., Ph.D. and Andrew S. Wright, M.D., *Basics of Cognitive Therapy*, http:/mindstreet.com/mindstreet/cbt.html

13 Paul H. Ray and Sherry Ruth Anderson, *The Cultural Creatives: How 50 Million People Are Changing the World* (New York: Harmony, 2000), p. 27.

14 Robert Bork, *Slouching Towards Gomorrah: Modern Liberalism and American Decline* (New York: HarperCollins, 1996), p. 23.

15 Stephen and Robin Larsen, *The Fashioning of Angels: Partnership as a Spiritual Practice* (West Chester, PA: Chrysalis Books, 2000), pp. 129-130

16 Quoted in Robert Herbert, Goodbye to All That, *The New York Review of Books*, November 4, 1999, p. 28.

17 Charles Frankel, *The Democratic Prospect* (New York: Harper Colophon, 1962), p. 181. In those same acknowledgements, he thanked me and my sister for adjusting "uncomplainingly to the tendency of their father to disappear into a brown study," and my mother for "editorial assistance (that) has come close to complicity in the crime."

18 Neil Postman, *Technopoly: The Surrender of Culture to Technology* (New York: Alfred A. Knopf, 1992), p. 13.

19 Thomas Berry, *The Great Work: Our Way Into the Future* (New York: Bell Tower, 1999), p. 29.

20 Estimates of the value of the annual marijuana crop range from $4 billion to $25 billion, making it quite possibly the largest cash crop in the US. Eric Schlosser, *Reefer Madness: Sex, Drugs and Cheap Labor in the American Black Market* (Boston: Houghton Mifflin, 2003), p. 14.

21 Ann Goodman and Peter Knight, Lobbying the Lenders, *Tomorrow Magazine*, July/August 1999, p. 14.

22 *Webster's New Universal Unabridged Dictionary*, p. 1439

23 http://www.faculty.de.gcsu.edu/~rviau/mythlecture.html.

24 The extent to which this was done naively, or symbolically, or as a convenient smokescreen for occult spiritual practices that defied Christian doctrine, seems to have varied depending on the alchemist. According to one commentary, the "balance of 'inner' and 'outer' work varied from alchemist to alchemist, from the 'puffers' who wanted to make gold quickly, to the adepts who saw it as a spiritual pursuit: '(T)here were always a few for whom laboratory work was primarily a matter of symbols and their psychic effect. As their texts show, they were quite conscious of this, to the point of condemning the [more literally-minded] goldmakers as liars, frauds, and dupes.' (Jung, 1998: 284).'" http://www.altsense.net/library/factual/megan/jung_x.html.

25 As I was doing final edits on this section, an announcement about a new magazine called *Organic Style* came across my desk. Calling itself 'Your ultimate guide to a balanced life,' it invited the reader to 'discover the meaning and purpose of your life,' 'find satisfaction and fulfillment,' and 'make a home that's comfortable and peacable.' Articles on the cover included 'What's really in your milk?,' 'Your Peaceful Home,' and '10 Tantric Sex Secrets.'

26 B. Joseph Pine II and James H. Gilmore, *Welcome to the Experience Economy*, Harvard Business Review, July/August 1998, p. 97

27 Ibid., p. 99

28 Michael Hill, *Theme drives auto dealership*, Kingston Daily Freeman, August 2, 1999, p. D1. Also see www.armorycenter.com.

29 http://www.news.cornell.edu/releases/May99/Butterflies.bpf.html

30 http://www.gamblingmagazine.com/articles/22/22-64.htm

31 Chistopher Lasch, *The Culture of Narcissism: American Life in an Age of Diminishing Expectations* (New York: Warner Books, 1979), pp. 29-30.

32 Robert Bork, *Slouching Towards Gomorrah: Modern Liberalism and American Decline* (New York: HarperCollins, 1996), p. 4.

33 Ibid., pp. 4-5.

34 Ibid., p. 5.

35 Ibid., p. 8.

36 Ibid., p. 3.

37 Ibid., p. 28.

38 http://www.lp.org/intro/

39 Michael Lerner, *The Politics of Meaning: Restoring Hope and Possibility in an Age of Cynicism* (Reading, MA: Addison-Wesley, 1996), p. 56.

40 Theodore Roszak, *The Voice of the Earth: An Exploration of Ecopsychology* (New York: Touchstone, 1992), p. 320.

41 Ibid., p. 273.

42 This is the point Ken Wilber is making when he condemns what he calls the 'pre/trans fallacy,' the misperception that the sort of behavior

Roszak has in mind represents emotional progress ('trans') when it is actually regressive ('pre'). "The new age enthusiasts, such as Roszak ... in their understandable haste to move beyond ego, ... frequently fail to specific clearly which direction that movement is or should be occurring. Two things then tend to happen: They either elevate pre-egoic license to the status of transegoic freedom (as the 'dharma bums' did), or they simply denigrate the role of mind, ego, secondary process and logic, and in its place argue for a mode that is called simply 'nonegoic,' 'nonrole bound,' 'nonlogical,' and so on. In such cases, this 'nonegoism' usually conceals a mixture and confusion of pre-egoic fantasy with transegoic vision, of preconceptual feelings with transconceptual insight, of prepersonal desires with transpersonal growth, of pre-egoic whoopee with trans-egoic liberation. Jack Crittenden, in a long and thoughtful review of this whole stance, concluded, 'It seems that Roszak, along with many other chroniclers of the Aquarian Age, misconstrues ego license for eco transcendence.'" Ken Wilber, *Eye to Eye: The Quest for a New Paradigm* (Shambhala: Boston, 1996), pp. 214-215.

43   http://www.cnn.com/2002/ALLPOLITICS/09/23/time.president.tv/

44 See www.rprogress.org/progsum/nip/gpi/gpi_main.

45 Randall Mason, *Economics and Heritage Conservation: Concepts, Values, and Agendas for Research*, in Economics and Heritage Conservation: A Meeting Organized by the Getty Conservation Institute, December 1998, p. 2.

46 Ibid., p. 2.

47 "Colleges derive predictions of applicants' performance from regression equations based on the performance of the previous year's students. The ability to predict freshman grades is the backbone of the SAT's claim to measure aptitude. In the world of psychometrics, the valid aptitude test is one that can predict a person's performance. A perfect prediction would be 100% accurate. A physical measurement, such as that provided by a thermometer or a ruler, generally delivers accuracy of 95% or more. The SAT, according to figures compiled by Ford and Campos of ETS, ranges in accuracy from 8 to 15% in the prediction of freshman grade point average. This means that, on the average, for 88% of the applicants (though it is impossible to know which ones) an SAT score will predict their grade rank no more accurately than a pair of dice." Glen Elert, *The SAT: Aptitude or Demographics?*, E-World, http://hypertextbook.com/eworld/sat.shtml#statistics.

48 Gloria Steinem, Foreword to *The Vagina Monologues*, by Eve Ensler (New York: Villard, 1998), p. xv.

49 http://radio.cbc.ca/programs/ideas

50 Thomas Berry, *The Dream of the Earth* (San Francisco: Sierra Club Books, 1988), p. 123.

51 Personal communication, November 19, 1999

52 Personal communication, December 10, 1999.

53 Personal communication, July 1999.

54 David Brooks, *Bobos in Paradise: The New Upper Class and How They Got There* (New York: Simon & Schuster, 2000), p. 269).

55 Orr made this observation at a conference sponsored by *Resurgence Magazine* and held at the Omega Institute in Rhinebeck, New York in September 2002.

56 Henderson's objections to emissions trading are not solely depth-dimensional. She also finds the concept badly flawed from an instrumental-reasoning perspective. "The incentives are perverse," she argues. "Emissions trading ends up rewarding polluting companies and doesn't reward companies that have radically reinvented what they do so that they no longer qualify for emission credits." Personal communication, September 29, 1999.

57 Georg Feurstein, *Toward a New Consciousness*, Noetic Sciences Review #07, p. 23, Summer1988, http://www.noetic.org/Ions/publications/review_archives/07issue07_23.html

58 http://www.integralage.com/scripts/catheader.asp?catid=12

59 http://www.integralinstitute.org/integral.cfm

60 Jack Crittenden, *What Is the Meaning of "Integral"?*, Introduction to Ken Wilber, *The Eye of Spirit: An Integral Vision for a World Gone Slightly Mad* (Boston: Shambhala Publications, 1997), p. x.

61 Personal communication

62 Personal communication, October 12, 2002

63 www.theworldcafe.com

64 www.commonway.org/cafes/CAFE1-1.html#notestop

65 www.commonway.org/cafes/CAFE1-1.html#notestop.For Abdullah, the Commons Cafes are only the beginning.He has set his sights on something bigger—the creation of a vast network of leaders who will collectively spearhead a transition to a world that works. "We're on a train headed south for destruction," he says. "We need to build a northbound train." Abdullah's Common Society Movement is deeply integral in nature. It is premised on inclusivity (this is the term he uses) and seeks to drive widepread consciousness change.

66 http://www.conversationcafe.org/join_main.html

67   http://www.nationalstrategy.com/nsr/v9n4Summer00/Salamon%20NGOs%20Summer%2000.htm

68 The ManyOne Network's structure and potential struck me as so enormous that in late 2002 I accepted a full-time job with the enterprise.

69 http://www.fourthsector.net/

70   http://www.newamerica.net/index.cfm?sec=about&pg=overview&static=Yes

71 Ted Halstead and Michael Lind, *The Radical Center: The Future of American Politics* (New York: Anchor, 2001), p. 16.

72 Ibid., p. 16.

73 Ibid., p. 208.

74 Personal communication, October 11th, 2002

75 Halstead and Lind, op.cit., p. 33.

76 Ibid., p. 64.

77 Ibid., p. 64.

78 Ibid., p. 64.

79 Personal communication, October 11th, 2002. *The Radical Center* cites polls conducted in 2000 by the Gallup Organization: "In a poll conducted January 26-26, 37 percent of respondents self-identified as independent, versus 32 percent Democrat and 30 percent Republican. In polls conducted on June 22-25 and December 13, the share of independents rose to 39 percent and 42 percent, respectively." Ted Hal-

stead and Michael Lind, *The Radical Center: The Future of American Politics* (New York: Anchor, 2001), p. 229.

80 Personal communication, February 9th, 2002

81 In addition to the usual specters of nuclear apocalypse and ecosystem collapse, we can add a third extinction scenario: that emerging technologies such as genetic engineering and nanotechnology will get out of hand and destroy the ecological basis for life on Earth. This possibility was raised in a headline-grabbing *Wired* magazine article by Sun Microsystems founder William Joy. http://www.wired.com/wired/archive/8.04/joy.html

82 http://www.rmi.org/sitepages/pid157.php

83 *Poll: Trust in corporations waning.* http://www.usatoday.com/money/2002-07-15-trust-poll_x.htm

84 *Business Week/Harris poll. How Business Rates: By the Numbers.* http://www.businessweek.com/2000/00_37/b3698004.htm

85 Aaron Bernstein, Too Much Corporate Power?, *Business Week*, September 11, 2000, http://www.businessweek.com/2000/00_37/b3698001.htm

86 Claire Cozens, McDonald's and Coke Fund Healthy Eating Drive, *The Guardian*, June 14, 2002, http://media.guardian.co.uk/marketingandpr/story/0,7494,737401,00.html

87 In a report written for Claros Consulting for a group of dissident ExxonMobil shareholders, Mark Mansley wrote, "In years to come, the legal costs could amount to between $200 million-$1 billion if the tobacco industry is any guide." He also estimated that if oil companies were held liable, total damages could exceed $100 billion.

88 James Hillman, *The Thought of the Heart and the Soul of the World* (Dallas: Spring Publications, 1992), p. 66.

89 Ibid., p. 67.

90 Wendell Berry, *Life Is a Miracle: An Essay Against Modern Superstition* (Washington, DC: Counterpoint, 2000), p. 45.

91 Erich Fromm, *To Have or To Be?* (New York: Bantam, 1981), p. 3.

92 *Charles Frankel Discusses Philosophy with John Fischer*, The Academic Recording Institute, 1959.

93 Ibid.

94 http://www.britannica.com/bcom/eb/article/7/0,5716,49927+1+48766,00.html?query=logical%20positivism

95 Aldous Huxley, *Island* (New York: Harper & Row/Perennial, 1962), pp. 275-276.

96 Ibid., p. 276.

97 Frankel, op.cit.

The author, his sister Susan and their father
-Lesconil, Brittany (Fr), 1954

Carl Frankel

Carl Frankel has been specializing in issues relating to sustainable development for close to two decades. He is a senior columnist with the magazine *green@work*, was the founder, editor and publisher of the trade newsletter *Green MarketAlert*, and has served as North American editor for *Tomorrow* magazine and contributing editor to *Yes! The Journal of Positive Futures*. He also works closely with The ManyOne Network, a start-up, socially responsible web portal service provider.

His 1998 book, *In Earth's Company: Business, Environment and the Challenge of Sustainability*, has been called "the best book I have seen about the business aspects of sustainable development" (David Buzzelli, ex-co-chair, President's Council on Sustainable Development).

Frankel's parents were murdered by burglars in 1979. His father, Charles Frankel, was a prominent professor of philosophy at Columbia University who embodied the secular humanist ideal for many people. While writing this book, the author often imagined himself in dialogue with his father about our cultural challenges and trajectory.

Frankel is a graduate of Princeton University (1970) and the Columbia University School of Law (1974). He serves on the Board of Directors of the Buckminster Fuller Institute and is a member of the Society of Environmental Journalists.

Frankel lives in Kingston, New York with his wife Deborah Bansemer and his cat Otis.

FOR MORE INFORMATION:
www.carlfrankel.com
www.outofthelabyrinth.com